TROIA

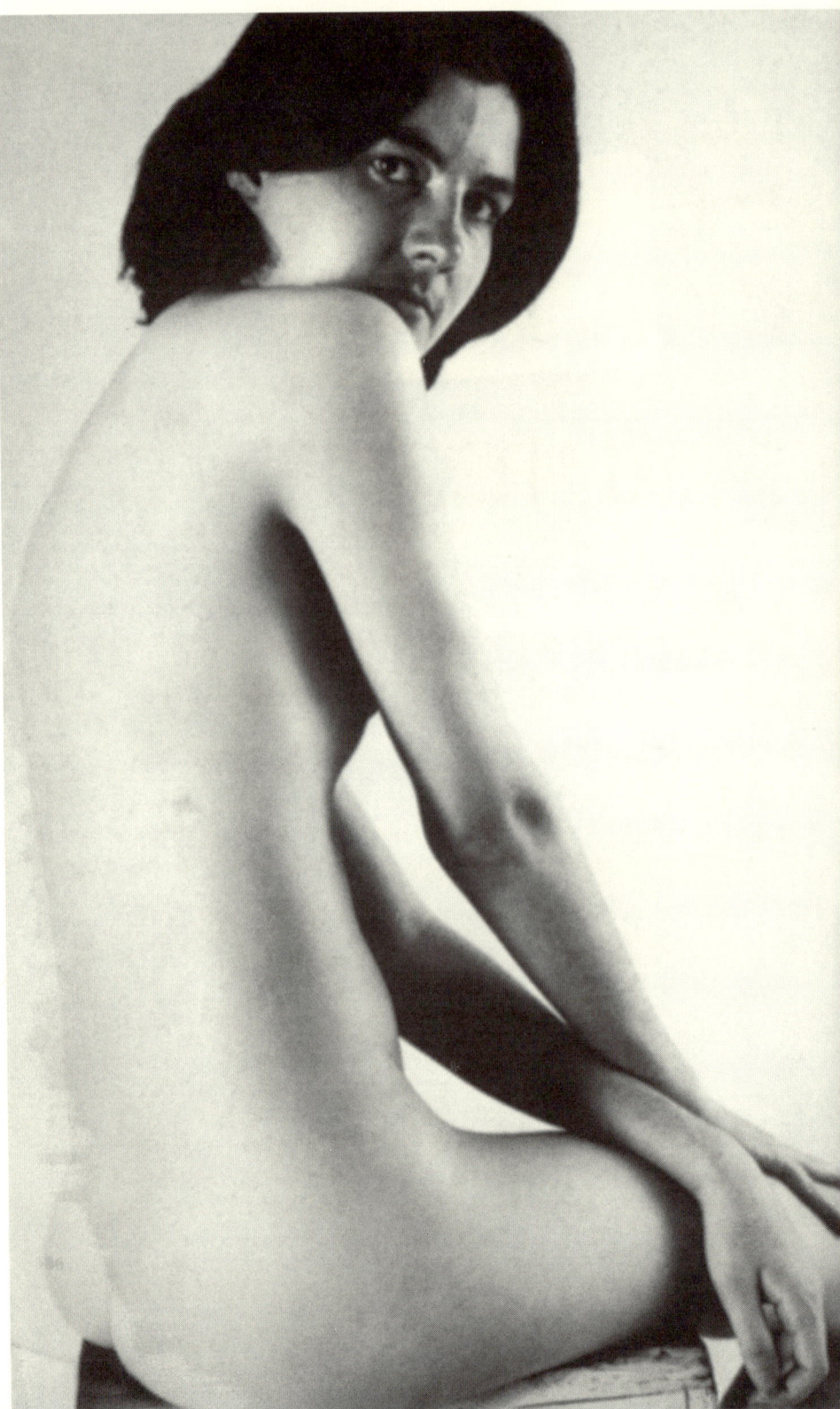

Troia
MEXICAN MEMOIRS

BONNIE BREMSER

Introduction by Ann Charters

Dalkey Archive Press
Champaign · London

Originally published by Croton Press, 1969
Copyright © by Bonnie Bremser, 1969
Introduction copyright © by Ann Charters, 2007
Cover art copyright © by Estate of Alice Neel
First Dalkey Archive edition, 2007
All rights reserved

Library of Congress Cataloging-in-Publication Data

Bremser, Bonnie, 1939-
Troia : Mexican memoirs / Bonnie Bremser. -- 1st Dalkey Archive ed.
    p. cm.
Originally published: New York, Croton Press, 1969.
ISBN-13: 978-1-56478-480-3 (alk. paper)
ISBN-10: 1-56478-480-0 (alk. paper)
1. Bremser, Bonnie, 1939- 2. Bremser, Ray. 3. Prostitutes--Mexico--Biography. I. Title.
HQ151.A5B7 2007
306.74'2092--dc22
[B]
                                                    2007026630

Bonnie Bremser by Alice Neel (1963, ink on paper, 29½ x 22 inches)
used by permission of the Estate of Alice Neel.
Photograph of Bonnie Bremser by Bernard McCaffrey
used by permission of the artist.

Partially funded by a grant from the Illinois Arts Council,
a state agency, and by the University of Illinios, Urbana-Champaign

www.dalkeyarchive.com
Printed on permanent/durable acid-free paper and bound
in the United States of America

INTRODUCTION

In August 1970 I met Bonnie Bremser when I stayed at Allen Ginsberg's farm in Cherry Valley, New York. A quietly beautiful woman about my age with dark hair and a shy smile, she was living at the farm with her husband, the Beat poet Ray Bremser, and their small daughter Georgia. It was shortly after they had returned from a disastrous trip to Guatemala. After Allen had introduced us, I asked how old Georgia was and discovered that she'd been born in the same month and year as my three-year-old daughter Mallay. This coincidence made me feel as if Bonnie and I had something very important in common, but I had felt a definite sense of sympathy with her even before I came to the farm. I had read her memoir *Troia* when it was published the year before, and I had thought that it was a unique book. The passage of more than a quarter of a century hasn't altered my opinion. I still believe that *Troia* is the most extraordinary memoir ever written by a woman in the Beat circle.

Brenda Frazer became Bonnie Bremser at the age of nineteen on March 21, 1959, six weeks after dropping out of Sweet Briar College and three weeks after meeting Ray Bremser at a party held in Washington following a reading that featured Allen Ginsberg, Peter Orlovsky, Gregory Corso, LeRoi Jones, and Bremser. Bremser was considered one of the Beat group, but he had served six years in the

Bordentown Reformatory after being convicted of armed robbery as an eighteen-year-old.

Though Bonnie didn't feel close to her parents, her father had loved classical music and was a frustrated writer, and he had given her the sense that literature was important. There's a touching moment at the end of *Troia* when she returns briefly to her father's house in July 1961 after several searing months with Ray in Mexico, and she mentions that her father makes her feel guilty about her "actual lack of creative energy." She needn't have felt so guilty. The last page of her memoir is dated October 11, 1964, and her creative energy overflows in the words that have transformed her down-and-out experiences in Mexico into art.

What made Bonnie become a writer? The epigraph to *Troia* is "Damn the pain; it must be written." She tells us why she writes in the book itself: "Do I have to tell this story on into the night, telling away the sickness?" "Because my faith in life had begun to fail." In her opening words, she explains that

> in looking back, what's important is not the technique or lack of it, but those few minutes when you overcome the frustration, bridge the gap, and hold something incredibly beautiful to you: the point where you don't see yourself anymore but you are there, and OBOY, that's the way you really are.

In the fall of 1961, a few months after Bonnie joined Ray in New York City after their return from Mexico, he was convicted on a new charge of robbery and sentenced to one to three years in a New Jersey prison, with a fourth year added for violation of his parole on an indictment for an earlier robbery that Bremser swore he did not commit. While he was in prison, Bonnie decided to write her memoir as if she were writing letters to her husband. He suggested the title, which he roughly translated for her as "courtesan." Ray also told Bonnie that he associated the word "Troia" with the ancient city of Troy, and that he thought of his beautiful wife as a powerful temptress like Helen of Troy. Bonnie herself associated the word with the feeling of being adventurous.

At this time Bonnie was still very much in love with Ray. As she wrote in *Troia*, "My heart belonged to Ray since the day I met him in Washington, that is the basis of my life, and all life before that can only be explained this way: that my heart knew that Ray was on his way to me." As she waited for her husband to be released from prison, Bonnie lived on the Lower East Side of Manhattan in a small apartment she found through the poet Clive Matson. As she describes it, the place was

> on Avenue A between 11th and 12th Streets, just one room with a tiny bedroom, a courtyard apartment back from the street so I didn't hear traffic noises. It was a perfect writing apartment. I had just stopped using heroin, which is very suppressive on your psyche, so I was feeling a burst of creative energy. I smoked massive amounts of marijuana while I wrote *Troia*. I grew my own marijuana on the windowsill—very wholesome stuff—and just smoked it up.

Bonnie had never attempted to write a book before she began *Troia*, and the earliest chapters of her memoir describe how she met Ray in Washington, D.C. and moved as his impressionable wife to Greenwich Village where he read his poetry at the Gaslight while she worked as a waitress to support them before they went to Mexico. Two of these introductory chapters, written in a conventional style, are included in the Penguin anthology *Beat Down to Your Soul* (2001): "The only job I could get [in the Village] was at the Cafe Bizarre. I was very unhappy about it but I was coerced. 'How are we going to eat?' And I couldn't argue with that." After these early chapters, the memoir continues in a different, consciously free style when Bonnie starts to describe the terrible things that began to happen to her and her husband in Mexico in the early months of 1961. *Troia* begins at the point when Ray had violated the terms of his New Jersey parole, and the couple was on the run.

Book One opens abruptly with the arrival of Bonnie and Ray and their baby daughter Rachel in Matamoros at the Mexican border. Here the prose seems to lift off the page, infused with Bonnie's emotional suffering and her sense of spiritual abandonment. In Matamoros the couple buy bus tickets to Mexico City, heading for Veracruz where they plan to stay with the Beat poet Philip Lamantia. Riding with her crying baby on her lap, Bonnie describes what she sees out the window as their bus approaches Mexico City: "I look out and God drops from his hand the myriad stars and constellations I have never seen before, plumb to the horizon flat landed out beneath the giant horoscopic screen of the Mexican heaven." The reader is suddenly aware that we have arrived in Kerouac country, the author whose literary style Ray Bremser admired above all others in the wild group of poets who had befriended him in New York City. Bonnie had met Kerouac only once. She'd read *On the Road* a short time after it was published in 1957, before she'd met Ray, and she'd fallen under the spell of the book. As she remembered, "I picked it up in a college bookstore and felt something was happening and wanted to be a part of it." After her marriage to Ray, she became one of the "mad ones," the fugitives and rebels whose lives Kerouac celebrated in his novel. Writing *Troia*, Bonnie took as her model the memoir *Doctor Sax* (1959)—her favorite of Kerouac's books—about his fantastic adventures in Lowell as a young adolescent. She wasn't acquainted with Kerouac's list of rules for his method of writing spontaneous prose, which Ginsberg had pinned to his wall in San Francisco as his guideline before beginning *Howl* several years earlier. Instead, Bonnie followed her instinct in using Kerouac's writing method. She was fascinated by the opening sentences of *Doctor Sax*, where Kerouac fixed his attention on the sidewalk in Lowell and let his memories of boyhood spin off from there: "Describe the wrinkly tar of this sidewalk, also the iron pickets of Textile Institute, or the doorway ... and don't stop to think of words when you do stop, just stop to think of the picture better." Creating the four chronological sections of *Troia*, Bonnie wrote while she smoked the marijuana from her own plants, drifting back into her memories and consciously letting "something visual prompt the writing," as she later told me.

The critic Michael Perkins recognized that *Troia* is "one of the few prose narratives by a woman besides Diane di Prima's *Memoirs of a Beatnik* [1969] to come out of the Beat literary movement." But di Prima had written about her experiences tongue-in-cheek as a pornographic work-for-hire. In 1953 Kerouac appropriated his lover Alene Lee's story of her mistreatment by her Beat lovers and her subsequent mental breakdown into his autobiographical narrative *The Subterraneous* (1960), and two years later in *Tristessa* (1960) he described the suffering of a morphine-wracked prostitute in Mexico City. With *Troia*, Bonnie became the only woman in the Beat group who had actually lived on the edge and come back to write a heartfelt book about it. As Bonnie learned in Mexico after many months of drug-taking (pot, coke, alcohol, magic mushrooms, peyote, and Benzedrine) while hustling among "Mexcity low life, milling no-goods of the streets" in order to support Ray while he wrote his poetry, "Being bitter is a means of holding your head up when you are too low for anything else to help; then usually, if you have any heart, you can build things up from there." Back in New York City, Kerouac's writing method gave Bonnie the approach to take when she relived her heartbreaking experiences in order to write about them. Instinctively she followed Kerouac's "Essentials of Spontaneous Prose," beginning with the "set-up" of memory and continuing by sketching the "undisturbed flow from the mind of personal secret idea-words, blowing (as per jazz musician) on subject of image."

When I recall my own reaction to *Troia* when I first read it so many years ago, I feel like alerting the unwary reader by repeating the words that William Carlos Williams used to conclude his introduction to Ginsberg's *Howl and Other Poems*. The older poet advised, "Hold back the edges of your gowns. Ladies, we are going through hell." Bonnie's honesty and courage in holding on to what was hers is exemplary. Not only did she survive her tumultuous Mexican adventure and write brilliantly about it—"I am alone, lonely, bugged, feeling more and more unloved, as if each trick I turn is a negative score on the happiness list"—but in 1997 she also made contact with the daughter she was forced to abandon as an infant.

The first edition of Bonnie's memoir was published by Croton Press in 1969 with the title *Troia: Mexican Memoirs* and republished as *For Love of Ray* by London Magazine Editions in 1971. Not long afterwards Bonnie decided that she couldn't continue her relationship with Ray. They separated in the early 1970s and divorced in 1976. Then in a remarkable turn-around, she went back to college and had a career as a soil scientist, working for fifteen years with the Progressive Soil Survey of the United States Department of Agriculture. Now retired, she laughingly says, "I like bragging about being a career woman." Bonnie has continued to write and will soon publish two small new books, one about her adventures with Ray in Guatemala and the other about her experiences in Cherry Valley and on Ginsberg's farm, where I first met her.

Created during a restorative time of tranquility on the Lower East Side, *Troia* captures the "unspeakable visions of the individual" describing what were perhaps the most harrowing months of her life. Becoming the quintessential Beat woman writer in her memoir, Bonnie first follows and then confronts the Beat aesthetic: "What are these legends growing in my head? All of it is about to fall out completely on the page." You be the judge.

Ann Charters, 2006

"Damn the pain; it must be written."

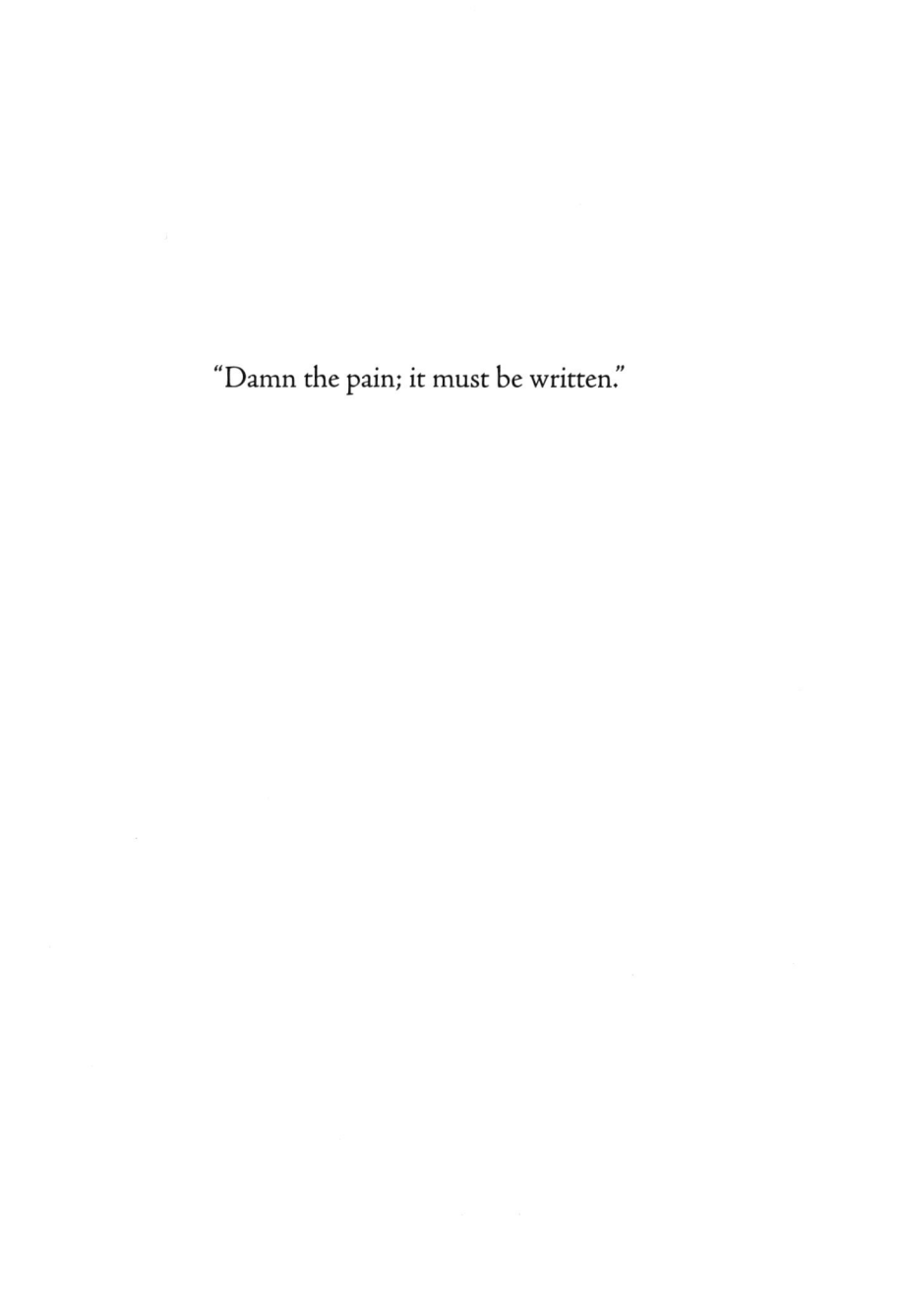

Contents

Book One
MEXICO CITY TO VERACRUZ AND BACK TO TEXAS
9

Book Two
MEXICO TO LAREDO: GETTING RAY OUT OF JAIL
77

Book Three
MEXICO CITY AND RURAL EXCURSIONS:
LOSING RACHEL
121

Book Four
MEXICO CITY AND BACK TO NEW YORK
179

. . . First off I want to tell a few really important things about me. I know that continuity is necessary, and I do my best up to a point, but I believe in distortion—I believe that if you get to a place where something is taking shape and want badly to comprehend the thing that you have created, supposedly for yourself (since everything is personal anyway), then any old thing to fill the gap will do—and that is the point where you come in . . . in looking back, what's important is not the technique or lack of it, but those few minutes when you overcome the frustration, bridge the gap, and hold something incredibly beautiful to you; the point where you don't see yourself anymore but you are there, and OBOY, that's the way you really are. . . . Here is the way I really am: I HAVE GOT PLENTY OF NOTHING, if you will excuse my banality. My heart belonged to Ray since the day I met him in Washington, that is the basis of my life, and all life before that can only be explained this way: that my heart knew that Ray was on his way to me. My heart has a mind of its own—and, speaking of minds, this is where I want to explain me: I have a dirty mind.

My mind is on my needs. I walk down the street and feel the thigh within my raincoat warmed by the sun. I like to think of other people helping me. It occurs to me that everything will be O.K. because there will always be someone to help me get the things that I want. I like the people who help me, as a rule, because their existence adds to the thought that everything is going to be O.K.

When I have no money I am able to desire vividly the things that money can buy. I look at them and am pleased at their availability; even looking at money pleases me. With a dime I walk into a restaurant and take a long time over a cup of coffee and am pleased to see people buying things that I don't have the money to buy, and a green bill passing hands is especially beautiful to me. A person sitting next to me complains of the food and the proprietor calmly throws it in the garbage and when the man leaves he pays for it, though he is not asked to, and leaves a tip for which the proprietor thanks him. I find them both admirable.

Walking by a wholesale jewelry store I am called into a dream by the fairy-tale beauty of diamond bracelets, and moreover, I think of the people I could have buy me those things; nothing more than that, the moment passes, but leaves its impression of a completed sensual experience. I decide that I will go without money more often to enjoy this feeling: the anticipation of confidence, the lilting dream which grows upon itself is a reality I had not expected to encounter.

I am pleased at my lack of clothing. My nakedness is anticipated much more in dreams than my eyes can ever plan for it in covering, and the means to the dream is a whole other dimension I hesitate to describe. The ideal covering for my body is sunlight, and in sunlight I will be admired (foremost by myself)—the afternoon sun I while away thus with my dirty mind.

Oh yes, but I can lay it down gently, too, at any stage, for I have changed, remember? The first time that Ray was taken away from me by New Jersey I was fresh out of college, married to Ray only six months, a rebel, yes, but still investigating just the outermost bounds of myself. I didn't know much of what anything was about, had only the confidence to accept Ray's love and marry him. That part was unmistakable, I was plenty old enough for that, but to deal with prisons and disappearances? You see, I must always do everything on my own. Though I am sometimes inspired, I am seldom advised, except, newly, then, by Ray. I thought that marriage was an end to all my problems, but it was more than that; it was a new life, and that I had to work my way through six months of it as isolated as I had been previously all my life, with little encouragement and little direction of my own, was a tragedy. The hope of a dream had long since died in my cynicism, and despair had taken over, enabling me to live in abandon without even knowing what abandon was. But the dream had grown freshly when I met Ray, and when they took him from me the first time, I abandoned my hope and gave up the faithfulness and the dream I had so implicitly believed in. But I was more unhappy than I had ever been, and that is a consolation, that is hope and some kind of recognition, though I knew it alone and had no idea that Ray felt the same way—the same as when I was constantly away from my mother in childhood. I thought that she didn't care, didn't even think about me when we were apart; I thought that I was the only lonely soul in the world, and accepted it, lived with it all my life, and when a chance came for companionship and good healthy exercise, I jumped on it. So, blame me! I can't blame myself anymore, for the repentance is done in the act and working through it.

The very night that they took Ray away from me, I capped the disillusion myself and pretended to find love everywhere, not only in the person of my real love. This is life, this is one of the drawbacks of living in a world so full of people and human beings—to find out that I'm not alone, in order to find out how truly alone I am, and then to be surprised to find out that I'm not alone after all—and take it all into my hands finally and weed out the garden, put down my mother and my father and my sister and everyone who would make me part of the family except my very individual axis, which miraculously is part dream and part real.

It all comes back to me: I was sure after marriage that Ray had made a bad bargain in me. I was afraid that if I wasn't worthy of him that maybe he wasn't good enough for me, by some quirk. Not knowing the worth of either of us sent me out to test the whole business. I tried seduction to see if I could pick up that one and lay him down again and try and investigate mindfully if the ones I was able to catch were worth catching. I cannot give a final opinion; as a rule, I got fucked over, that's what the world does to trusting people. Yet, it was all between Ray and me, so no harm was done. As soon as I knew that Ray was coming back, that there was no end to things, though New Jersey fucked over him worse and took him away and gave him back—the same as those unthinking males I fucked while he was gone—we were only washed around by the waves, and when time got turned on again, we both coolly moved to each other's sides to start it all over again.

Yes, funny, you who know me, Bonnie of the streets, of the hard touch, of the frantic spiritual judgment come to coerce you, you remember, jazz, soul, bebop, and well along the straight road to salvation. Funny that I should come so late, so weak and confused to explain the basis of it all, to fall back on the poetic pattern, spoken rivets on a plank. Lord, let me keep on with the patter. Come now to save me, phony this, the means—but the end? That's what I wonder mostly.

 I have lied. I am ashamed of my fear, afraid to disclose my lack of scruples. Oh, I am inscrutable, too, even to myself, and don't think, oh reader and thrill seeker, that that ain't the real payback—the man inside hibernated for a long winter, how to dig him out and now look it in the face. Don't I have a right to fear my own frightened sensibilities first, before yours? It's only natural, I take the responsibility; learn that we and society will get along O.K. Should I invoke the muse? No, that would be an excuse. Or should I cite history about the temple prostitutes? No, that would be a downright lie. Tell you straight? I'm getting to it—you wait, for a change, you drags, you barriers who want to shelter me from the purity of my own *action* by layers and walls of shitty, philosophical drag. Call me an addict ... huh, if so, you yourself are the drug, a drug and a drag, all of us wallowing in it now, but I intend to clear the atmosphere at least for my own breathing. That's how much I care for your morals—clear enough? *Get off* my back—*I will moan and groan in misery no more.*

 My soul is black to its depth and the heart shines through like a beacon, or that powerful Egyptian self-induced light which moves all material things effortlessly. The pacified ghost roams at leisure within the pyramid, takes on the countenance of its own sphinx, expresses itself inwardly, and that pretty much excludes you.

Book One

MEXICO CITY TO VERACRUZ AND BACK TO TEXAS

Once across, we were quickly tired of Matamoros and purchased tickets to Mexico City. Transportes Del Norte, maroon buses, nothing to complain of in these first-class accommodations, we had enough money to get safely to Mexico City from where we were somehow to get safely to Veracruz, where we were to find our refuge . . . had I already exchanged one fear for another? Had the cold damp night of Matamoros put another chill into my heart? Was my fear at this time all composed of not being able to handle external circumstances, afraid I would not be able to keep Rachel healthy, or at least not crying (and that was a feat I didn't often succeed in), and not to be able to satisfy Ray—what was happening in his head, something similar? And it all was so extremely personal, this service of responsibility, that the failure of it and maybe the success I have not had much chance to experience up to this point was a very lonely thing; we were not really helping each other too much now. Each of us was just clinging as well as possible to what shreds of strength were left in the confidential self. The bus ride to Mexico City, full of this, I am constantly with the baby on my lap, broken-hearted at every spell of crying, the frustration of not being a very good mother really—trying to groove, trying to groove under the circumstances—and in spite of it I have impressions of dark-shrouded nights of passage through the hills, of an oasis of light in a restaurant stop. 2 A.M. with everyone sitting around the narrow lighted room—with a sense of it being the only lighted room for fifty miles around—eating eggs Mexican style for the first time. Ray got his *huevos rancheros* and I got eggs scrambled with fried beans and this was sort of a prelude to our Mexican trip. This meal in itself would come to be one of the great Mexican treats; eggs, how many places have we had those eggs I came to remember with great pleasure, but then, at that time, it was fear and anxiety not even to know how to ask for an egg in Spanish, and though I probably exaggerate now the lostness of not being able to make myself understood, I can now see that it was not just the language that caused the fear. Somehow the fear was cumulative, the desire growing as the inability increased.

The trip—a maroon bus awaits us beside the low immigration building, near the broken-down bridge—beer cans clatter in the dusty road afternoon; no sunlight but the approaching lowering clouds of a thunderstorm spreading out over the sky into gray vastness of a depressing standstill underneath any tree. Lonely, your reality here in Matamoros, the streets which carry through the center of town growing in importance to the four central parallels which cut out the square of the plaza, where afternoon *bistek*-eaters and shoeshine boys eye each other from across the unpaved streets; these same streets spread outward into the still mathematically correct city layout, but sidewalks disappear and houses rise in the midst of a block shacked upwards from a broken-down fence entryway by eroded paths. A house may take any shape or position within a block, and weeds of menacing aspect care little for the store on the corner so drawn into its cache of paper candies and orange soda signs it has shrunk to the stature of a poverty-struck doll house—the incredible ironies of Mexico—the wild-flung filth of Matamoros. Leaving town on the bus, mudhole crossroads fifty yards wide of rutting and industry—some International Harvester or reaping machine showroom with its economic splendor surveying the city; it will grow on, and the sky disapproves. Pass Sta. Teresa, a cafe faces east on the flat land. Look across to the Gulf, and nothing looks back, save the mesquite bushes; a mangy dog chases a couple of not-promising cows across a landscape you would not expect to carry even that much vision of life. Seen from the air, Transportes Del Norte carries on, a vision of good service, sixty people burning up the dust on the first stretch of the roads, which do indeed all lead to Mexico City-San Fernando, Tres Palos, Encinal. The sun shines briefly as I change the baby's diaper and we have a cup of coffee and head back to the bus. Santander Jiménez, we do not know yet that from here dots one of those "almost" roads perpendicular to the route of traveling civilization. A road which grows out of the solid surety of modern highway, dotting in weak secrecy into the plain to Abasolo where another almost not-to-be-seen road goes nowhere, but goes—we want to see where all the roads go, since then, but this first trip just gets us there and quick, gets us there where we are going, and we don't know yet that nothing waits but the bottom waiting to be scraped in our own whimsical and full-of-love fashion—got to get there and quick—damn the crying and wet diapers and laps full of Gerbers on the bus, of leg cramps and not much to view—Padilla, Guemez, Ciudad Victoria, chicken salad sandwiches and the unknown feeling of a waterfall. In all of these places we stop, passing through, rushing downward, seeking our level, slowly dying, get it over, let's get there. Ciudad Monte, nonstop Valles, passing in the night the bus driver picks up on lack of sleep, answers on the wheeling whispering pavement. We take our first curves into the hills, the roads start to swing—Tamazunchale, lights seen across a valley, Jacala, pencil marks on maps of future excitement. We turn east in the night approaching Ixmiquilpan, herald Indian feathers, the driver mutters incoherent names over the sleeping passageway, the bus careens as we shoot through Actopan, come another and final turning point at Pachuca. The driver announces the last lap and everyone stirs and gets excited at the news, not realizing it is more than three hours of approach to Mexico City. I look out and God drops from his hand the myriad stars and constellations I have never seen before, plumb to the horizon, flat landed out beneath the giant horoscopic screen of Mexican heaven.

Why do I hold back and hide, when I am sure at least of one person as understanding as I of my own faults and maybe as proud of our achievements? Oh yes, let's don't get personal about it at this late hour—had we done so earlier, tempestuous natures would have wracked to the lowest hill what now begins to be seen almost as a peaceful Arcadia we retire to, even in exile, now. . . .

Two o'clock *en la mañana*, we arrive in Mexico City and the bus leaves us off at ADO and not at the Transportes Del Norte bus terminal. In a swelter of homeless-appearing people whom we don't recognize there are many who are waiting for the morning bus perhaps, and though they look disreputable something will eventually be brought out of their packs to make them proud—like us, our records, our chevrons at that point, I guess, on our way to make the scene at P's and it couldn't be too soon for me. I was cold, tired, and ready for the new day to dawn with everything O.K., as usual. Taxi drivers, *caldo* eaters of the night, our soon-to-be compadres of doubtful reckonings on Mexico City taxi meters. When the meter registers two pesos, the passenger somehow must pay four and, even more surprisingly, we find out this is not just tourist graft and that the taxi in Mexico is one of the cheapest rides anywhere with privacy like a king; cheapest except for the bus ride, if you are game, but that is more rollercoaster thrills.

P was not at home. We walked, looking for a place to have coffee and get warm, for though we travel light we have the burdens of 300 miles in our heads. I remember now the opposite trip for me later when I flew from Mexico City to Washington in five hours and was dizzy for days afterward, unbelieving—and now I make the trip in my head, slowly, in pieces, this morning with the sun I climb the overhanging hills of Acapulco, alone, lonely, alone, full of the meaning of death, and life, either end of it, Mexico, Mexico, your sun crashes me in the head obliterating all bodily care, all shame, shameless Mexico, I am your child, and you have my child as the token.

Like the man who taps you on your waiting-for-hours shoulder, P finally comes to the window, ahh, relief, I give the baby a little jiggle for joy, ooyboy, baby, this is it, we enter. Five flights up, an imposing building, strange this is for us, even in a strange country. In Hoboken we live in houses of the renovated artist type, to put it politely. We live in ramshackle houses where we can and love it—modern apartment buildings for us, whafor? But I am tolerant for once, maybe even glad, I want to flake, a couple of hours of peace, unmoving. But there is no peace for our bodies, more food for the soul on top of all the rest, and maybe it is better, the truth, soul full of food in Mexico ... We turn on, do indeed at this point display our chevrons and for once they are appreciated, but we were used to that, Change of the Century, Ray Charles. We all were there at that first meeting, P, L, his blonde stage-managing wife, in bed asleep, no doubt working the next day, in spite of our cataclysmic arrival, but P knows and believes, as all groovy poets who dig us, no one otherwise could. We had met P in our marriage year, arriving in San Francisco on foot, having just aired our souls on the Mojave Desert. He took us to his room in the B Hotel and, handing us one enormous reefer, proceeded to read stuff that will knock you out, poetry that cannot fail to hit you in your own personal cause of it all, and therefore we love him, that is P, still, I believe. N was there, as I say, the whole Mexican crew, jive N, the first of the absconders, who had, I believe, invited us to Mexico in lieu of staying to testify at Ray's trial, whereby we would have had a double strength of truth on our side, but what does that matter, all visions of trial and parole past, have we not achieved our escape, have we not disembarked from it all and many mornings together in the waste of a life will prove it's no mistake. Salvage what you can, when there is no hope, run for your life, this is what I felt all along, the closing around the ears like a bad drug taking hold which has been administered involuntarily.

Melchior Ocampo in the morning light is not half so scary and we all retire to the nearby hip food stand and eat hamburgers and apple pie with ice cream and coffee. It is one of those great pot feasts that are always for all time remembered like some memorial along the road of our beautiful experiences. God praise marijuana, yes, my baby, I will never put you down. A few things stay close to our hearts, definitive, a happy to have a habit thing with no pain, no remorse, no sickness—although we did contact some people in Mexico who were

MEXICAN MEMOIRS

profound ex-postulants of LOCOS who had smoked too much (this was more a way of bragging that the pot you buy for an arm's-length thick amount costing less than a dollar is likely to shack you up until you decide to buy again), we have never had more than one or two disagreements with them, and that purely external, say for instance once or twice not having the minimum of survival and therefore having to do without, and only then, and then it was a frenzy to get straight and quick, and nothing wrong with that I guess. Sweet marijuana—lotus blossom I am entitled to call you now, being thoroughly a member of the club.

Ray was perhaps responding to the illusion of everything being beautiful. He always was ahead of me in that respect, and I do respect, although it in fact leaves me behind. He decided to stay in Mexico City for twenty-four hours more while it is decided for me that I will travel to Veracruz by bus with N and the baby. Ah bitter, I was not about to accept with grace my maidenly burdened-by-baby responsibility at this particular time. I should have put my foot down instead of being shuffled, because see what it did in rebellion (sure! almost sure! suspecting something really wrong since Matamoros—that Ray had already set his eye on something that didn't include me—what could it be—my perceptions were not sharp) and my survival reflexes were working overtime, I guess. But I go—midway between holding the baby on the eight-hour bus trip, the night quickly sets in and I decide to try my seductive powers on N, and the mistaken bluejeans, not to survive this episode, did indeed entice his hand where it should have by any standards stayed away from, the baby on my lap, we arrive in Mexico, me zipping up alone, my lonely pleasure, had I known I could have got in any restroom by my own mechanics—damn N. If

I could only do more than grab at a passing branch over my head, but the trouble with that is everything up until now has taken place fast on the go, the screeching terror of speed of everything falling out from underneath you—the recurring dream of bridges falling and falling away from beneath your very feet into rushing water, the resulting social shock, but more than that, knowing what it is to fall for the last time forever.

I set down in Veracruz, not I alone, me and the little me, Rachel, we arrive there escorted into taxicab jive and Veracruz barely registers our arrival. The American Consul is not informed, the DA knows not what is about to hit him, the FBI thinks that we are maybe laid up with a cold in Hoboken. And yet we are already doing the dance; the Paso Doble of passionate worth dissembles all other meaning of life and we dance, we all dance, Veracruzano's Negroes, the woman on the corner shakes her wet clothes into a floating heap on some not-so-precious patch of grass, gelatinas yelled through the streets, the palms again, all dancing dancing, the sun rises, Veracruz rises, some altar on this Easternmost coast, the morning of Mexico, Veracruz rises beyond the sugar fields. Oh Cordoba, the plaza dances, the streetcar certainly dances, this is the dance of the sun I have fallen into and knowing my own heart also at least dance, abide the sacrifice, it is unimportant, but dance. . . .

I thought everything was swell when the sun arose. I saw the woman across the way doing her morning wash, the shuttered door of N and his wife B's house on Calle Arista, but I missed Ray, still hassling in the German American Hotel? He tells me later an episode whereby he is locked out of his hotel room—now I remember I think, he wanted to write is why he stayed—I have somehow figured out in the night that if I think everything over well, collect all of the pieces of my travel-worn memory that I will find the truth, and the truth will be that Ray has done me no harm—and saying later that this is the point where I take on myself the responsibility and clean aside the shit so that the sun can shine. But Ray has not come back yet so this is all heartrending conjecture. I take care of baby Rachel, look out onto the tufted street, wash all day in the patio sunlight, getting the feeling. Besides, remember those were diaper days, Rachel somewhat settled being settled, the sweet little cherub face, Rachel, your story will come out as you awaken into the next month's mud puddles, we must get you a house, we must settle here in this beautiful land of Veracruz. There is no indecision, Mexico blacks out slowly the hurtsome parts of the brain. I go for a prophetic bus ride to the place where a young jiver in baggy pants, fixed suave style with bicycle clips asks me if I am waiting for someone—oh, the universe I am to grow accustomed to in Mexico. I am redeemed! In other words, I have got me an education.

Now we go by trolley car, overhanging the sides, Toonerville Trolley, Ray calls it, high on reefer we do not remember every street at all yet, but try to call them out by name to each other, laughing, cracking up all of glorious heavenly today to be hung up in a name, here we go—walking ponderous around the suspected snake holes (oh yes, the first day I take off, rebellious of my duties, through nearby and up the dunes to look at the other side, donkeys flounder in the sand and stinging bees and sickly weeds I stay around just long enough to find a snakeskin, uh oh, Toonerville wide, wide Missou do you come to my eye here, too? I am long enough in envy of some pythoness maybe I don't mind, have not yet seen my first Veracruz witch, which sight will make me question the blackness of my soul finally—a trophy on that hill) across the wide Netzaxihuatl, which should go unnamed, I do my human American best here, the wiser before, unnamed, catch the coming trolley at Zaragosa, the Zaragosa trolley, or the Matio Molino on Zaragosa—I can't remember which, bebop, the pot takes over and it's all just funny games, too, Toonerville Trolley, in fact, is true, and when the electricity goes off all over the city and the trolleys don't run—nobody turns on the radio to find out what's the matter that he can't get to work super fast, but Veracruzano style sits in each individual seat with each individual joint and each individual be cool, likewise, games, it's true! Truly! The museum which we finally pass near the Malecón, wall around the port, the historical marine Cortezian tourist museum of R, the hip landlord of N and B who is also the Man, the pot connection, only don't tell yet, for institutions are not quick to change in Veracruz and we want to go back yet, be cool, gringos, and wait for the electricity to come back on.

The little boy with big head fulla water and clubfoot to boot, the classic cripple on our block, Mexico is full of cripples, the little boy runs loose and teases us, evil crow voice full of croak and guttural sounds echoing the empty space of all that water splashing, confused he fits in sociologically and welcomes us three blocks out of sight. Gringos, not *oye gringo*, or *mira gringa*, but pure trumpeting the call for all mongrel dogs to come from their nest to greet gringos, Don Quixote in his colonialized domain has no match for this boy's sincerity, till he finally one day, overcome by the truth of his claim, throws rocks, gets beat, becomes leery and smiling and only throws from behind out of sight and runs to some secret hideaway or another territory where he bugs someone else for hours after an episode, period enough for things to cool down so they can get worse. The rest on the block stand to be seen with open hearts, their domestic hearth, which they do not defile with other than that ever, and maybe do not possess much more than that. I do not worry. We just want to be left alone, to get straight, we survive a couple of what we learn to call Del Nortes, the sun finally proceeds to shine for a couple of days of spring and Rachel greets the morning light squinty-eyed, the babe in all its encompassing beauty and complete expression draws all open hearts to it, an object of worship, our white baby. More so later, to my circumstantial chagrin, I find that intrigues of stealth surround the worship of this white baby, the black dance is done in caverns we don't know about yet, the smoke of another kind of hearthside, and yet the dance in its own rhythm, oh my soul, my Rachel, I will turn black to get you back....

This is not a time for thought, no poetical figures dancing in symbolic gesture to be remembered; the poetry is all depleted, the images so old and overused it is like the end of a lifetime. Everything is dragged out from the place where it has been consoling and laid down, lay it down, this is the end.

The three of us laid out on a tile floor, Del Norte blows under doors too casual for the security of weather-stripped United States comfort to believe at first, like a summer raincoat worn all winter uncaring. The baby sneezes, coughs, gets sick all over every day. N practices his horn in another room and it is a question of who gets bugged more over whose noises—the most unsuccessful experience at communal living in this not-very-well-built house. N and B had moved into it new, brand-new, and that may sound like a good thing, but unfortunately the house had not had a chance to dry out properly before the wet season had come and threw out all its damp vapors. I dream of the stove in Hoboken sending off warmth and expectation of endless comforts. Every time the sun shines just a little I am out into the patio, glad that it's all over already and then, around noon, the clouds gather and there is another day of winds, rain, and you would think it was a constant hurricane—great speculations among the populace about when the season will end. R knocks on the door about every morning, a friendly landlord call to see how everyone is doing, a joint passes from one or the other source. I am flattered to be included in the group, too shy to say much, resentful of our dependence on N and B. B is very domineering and pregnant, I am sure that N has told her how hot I was on the bus, they retire behind their private bedroom door regularly to fight. The house is rigged for summertime ventilation so that even when Ray and I are invited to sleep on a burlap (this is a kind of hair-shirt burlap) cot set up across from their door, everything is heard through holes out in the walls—including Rachel crying, twenty different times in the night, heard but unseen. I go to her in the absence of lights at Ray's orders to shut her up, or alone worried to bother our host and hostess so, I walk up and down for hours—the vigil with Rachel until dawn. I try to get some sleep during the day—Ray lies beside me for a few moments, back from the post office, maybe a couple of times we receive mail with small bits of money, but generally now mail is the news and he stays depressed, doesn't want me to touch him, much less any ardor of his own. I continue to wonder.

 I stand at the door with Rachel, looking out: Mexican children collect on the sidewalk to stare. In Mexico, the sidewalk is a part of the house to be washed every morning with the tile floors—how to be myself in such a different place? Put it all in a sieve and squash your personality through into a new diversified you—the process will take about four months. I would almost jump this gap for my own sake, sweep the floor, wash the diapers, go to the store to be repeatedly embarrassed by people who obviously do not want to have anything to do with you ("let the *Gringa* go first") I point at three hot sausages and some black and white cookies and run quickly home. Next time, I try to get Ray to go but he won't. We keep a constant watch on N and B; better try to cop a few pesos so we can all three eat. My head is threatened by the hopelessness of trying to keep alive under these conditions. Hang on! Where is my romance—where is the total image, even now I cannot see lifting backwards, the duality of something growing underneath all the misery, a new life indeed; wait till it makes a debut.

I know that this is a rotten way to keep everything in suspense. I am about to achieve my heart's longing. At the bottom of everything we are about to take another fall. I would even jump from a roof to make it all more explicit, but Veracruz is too low for that—about to realize how easy it is to adapt, and demonstrate it, once you recognize your surroundings. But first I had to jump away from Ray and blame it all on him.

I won't say we didn't try to get along with N and B; she would pick up her basket-weave pocketbook decisively and say, "Let's all go to Mocombo," and we would go, but how far apart we were from them. Even on the beach, though we would eat shrimps and drink beer together, I would be all for the other end of the beach which was simply wilderness and they would stick by the commercial stand, making it on beer. And, after all, they are $50 a week closer to civilization than us, and I develop an obvious dislike for her folksy woven shirts, and prefer my sun-browned nothings and am becoming outspoken that way. We try to make it running around to nearby bars and eating *panuchos* and listening to the jukeboxes as if we didn't have another care, but the couple of pesos is always quickly depleted. I prefer to walk into the ocean brave, be independent and unafraid—Ray watches me emerging from the water.

. . . *La Casa Del Cambio*—I am still hung on B's pocketbook, see it everywhere today in New York, New York in Mexico. B picks up her pocketbook when she is about to go out to shop and Ray is at the post office; it was a trip that took him three or four hours every day, understandably, nothing to come home to, but sometimes he showed up immediately with Mexican pesos, and we are off the ground, flying to the Perroquia for breakfast, maybe making plans to go to the beach, or more likely to the movies to see *Tarzan and Jane*. But usually nothing, he gets back about one or two, leaving me alone with N and B and the baby for hours, or preferably me alone completely. Then B brings back food which I feel guilty accepting and at the same time am incensed that she does not give full consideration to the needs of the baby, and that she will later look down her nose at me for doing so, in my own way.

One day, N went down to the Museum to see R (his regular jaunt), and comes back with news of a crazy redheaded Mexican who speaks English and is great. Later to be known as L, he arrives a few minutes behind N, and we see him coming from blocks away; as the Mexicans do us, he is so strange, an entourage of Mexicans under his command, he takes over in whatever area he cares to settle. "Wanna go for a ride in my car?" He orders some Mexican child he has officially adopted in the oil fields where he had made his not-too-legal killing, loaded, in fact, with money, the rumor goes, this boy worships his very funky person and leaps to every command. "Go get the car," the boy giggles and does not move. L shouts, "get the car, you son of a fucked whore dog." The boy cowers giggling, until L's wife gently reminds him that the car is still stuck, half underwater in the sand at Villa Del Mar, and doesn't he remember? No, he doesn't remember. Oh yes, it was those crazy Mexican *putos* that did it, making him drink all of that bad tequila—he'll fix them! So the kid is sent for a taxi instead, and everyone, except me and the baby, goes down to the beach to look at the car. Ray comes back later and is nice to me, teases me, plays with me, I get mad, probably try to make a scene and at the point at which I am in tears of complete frustration, complaining at being left behind and sick of the whole mess of our life, neglected poor poor me, he whips out a twenty which warms my heart a little but I turn up my nose, so I look again when he flashes it directly in front of my eyes I see it is an American twenty, 250 pesos, and I get scared thinking he has finally found a bank of something, but it turns out he has hit it off with L, of course, he would.

The next night we are out having fun for hours and then come home to cool it happy and high, with the baby Rachel content and well fed. B streams dramatically in the door crying that N has beat her up in the middle of a street nearby, frantic, and ready to leave him, she tells Ray (not a word to me) that N is drunk and she thinks he's going to kill her . . . And N coming into the house soon after does look like he's going to kill her. They start in on a fight like I have never seen before: first he shouts and curses and beats her around for a while, after which she cries uncontrollably lying on the floor till she quiets down and then (Good God! I think) she jumps up in a fury and grabs him around the neck with some kind of half nelson or something trying to strangle him, she gets the better of it for a while until he breaks loose and starts throwing furniture around and they scream at each other, things evening out; Ray referees. I have never seen such a disgusting fight—B pregnant and not caring, and N, completely berserk about something, finally turns to us, unashamed (B meanwhile on the floor again temporarily defeated), started out (to Ray), "you know what the dumb bitch did? She lost the baby! She had a miscarriage, she broke her water bag, she got on a horse—the goddamn dumb bitch got drunk and stole a policeman's horse. She went for a ride. I had to go find her and when I did, she was all wet, she told me she had broken her water bag. So I beat her up!" The whole story came out later that B had just had too much to drink and had peed all over herself down the policeman's saddle, which made N even madder (probably also to know that she was still pregnant) and he beat her up really, trying for the real thing, I guess. But we had left by that time, left them to enjoy it by themselves. We took the baby to a hotel in the market in Veracruz—to a room with two beds, which the hotel always loves because the second was for Rachel to wet on. That was our last involvement in N and B's household, a pleasant relief to be away. When I went back to pick up the baby's things, everything was back in the same domestic groove, except for the broken chairs and N's favorite memento, a hole in the door where his fist reportedly had gone through, but I don't believe it. N always had himself figured to be very tough.

We took up our abode in the Hotel P and Ray went right out and bought me an Indian skirt of green with black swirls and a sash of black, and the skirt was so long and full it was like something to dance in. I later hung it on a wall in our house because it made us both too self-conscious for me to wear it; it hung on the wall with my white Italian fan. I sat on the balcony overlooking the mercado while Ray was out, an enormous room with two huge windows opening onto the balcony—reality exerting myself to keep the baby content and to gain Ray's favor. As morning comes I buy two clay cups and get them filled with coffee at a nearby cafe for our breakfast.

On the beach at Villa Del Mar early in the morning Ray and I walked out to a point where the sand ends and the rocks cover the bottom of the water in mysterious green caves; we looked among the rocks on the point of land we were walking, searching among all the broken shells for whole ones. The wind is blowing everything cold, and the baby in my arms did not want to lie on the sand, I stood around happy, doing the same as Ray, and finally retired next to the high sea wall, cursing the sun that wouldn't shine and the sand that blew into the poor baby's eyes. It was so obvious she was uncomfortable that I tried to have fun with her in defiance of both our loneliness; Ray made a picture against the pale early morning light—thin, bent, surrounded by the water, the mast of a fishing boat passed behind him. I counted the time of its passage, waiting for others to appear, knowing that the fishing boat's placement was a measure of time in Veracruz. The dampness of the land promised rain—it is time to go—are you coming, Ray?—just another minute—another hour passes—we walked to the streetcar and got sent home while Ray went to visit the post office.

Or, Ray and Rachel and I start out to the post office early, going to have coffee at the Perroquia—morning breakfast place of businessmen, teenagers, husbands and wives, husbands and mistresses,

TROIA

American tourists, German tourists, Russian spies, and sailors passing through of all descriptions. Only Veracruz knows the reason for a restaurant to be named "barber shop" and Veracruz of all description passes by, crosses itself and kisses its fingers to the Virgin; the streetcar passes by amidst catcalls, a crazy bus revs beside it, and a race is on for the start at the next corner, pedestrians and passengers of no account, this contest acknowledged personal and also patriotic domain of drivers, uninsured perilous risks for the sake of the game. Two men across the corner wash the pavement of the Plaza in front of the Palacio Gobierno which is a Spanish dream of balconies and underwalking intrigues only now honored by slick shipping clerks on the make—the square-shaped park of the plaza slices into immaculate pie sections of bench backs and miniature trees twisting with symmetrical bald branches, houses a tiny fountain with colored tiles which is every morning emptied and cleaned for public use, for the cruisers' comfort, for drunken *boracheros*' collapse, and subsequent edification of tourists to the glory of Spain—but Veracruz is black—the whole town cleans its face scrupulously every morning—from the line of market-vicinity Guerrero whore-stalls to some unrecognized to all but the reverent mercantile-acknowledged palatial house, the preparations for the day are the same: throw water everywhere on the bared tiles, scrub, sweep, put everything back, stucco gleams wet with water in the rising sun, the monkishness of Indian dirt flavors the soul, but the topsides of everything are Christian and clean. Ray takes off across the plaza to the post office—a marimba band with drums and harp plays carnival waltzes, stops and starts, the tempo inspired by a coin's clank. I sit and dig it for free, amazed. Ray comes back and decides to go for a walk, sending Rach and me onto a bus where my melting backside is threatened destruction by the wooden bench's lurch as the jolting bus races around the plaza principal. Skidding on streetcar tracks, I relax with relief after we make the dangerous turn into the market section at unabated speed—Indians run from the ruthless drunken bus and I sit tense till the wind in the window grabs my attention. Rachel refuses to sit and wants us both to lose our heads over the passing scenery. Rachel, my hip little adventuress, so deserving of love and fun and everything we are about to get, though at great expense; damn the sacrifice.

Beyond the morning's darkness yet things begin to move about in the market, I have awakened to change Rachel's diapers and move to watch the nighttime Indians fade into the distance drunken, collapse up some alley, up many alleys they filter away just at the end of night, there is a half-hour pause where nothing moves—the market is closed down, corrugated steel doorways hide what was an open-air stall, someone's pushcart suffers a nighttime bicycle loot—the Mexican has something better than law and its pitiful enforcement, a sense of real desire to protect himself and the surrounding family and possessions including his own dignity, so therefore you do not find people getting away with threats and insults so much unnoticed as in the United States. Loss of something dear is not a vague unreality that the police will take care of if it is found to be illegal, but something you gotta watch out for yourself and find people caring for what is most close to them—somehow very real to me—somehow very much more than just the direction of responsibilities. . . . A market watchman guards the goods. The market roof overhangs the street and adjoining alley pagoda-like suggesting no life inside, the rats take a holiday, down the dark street of no opening door, solid adobe chute with corrugated negations of the daytime opening into infested netherworld like a popped kernel. I go back to sleep and wake into the dusty fury of another day's marketplace, the atmosphere of this hotel being a place where some hardware-merchant salesman coming in to close a deal from Xalapa one hour away might stay, certainly no tourist place this, but I remember it very romantically, Hotel P balcony looking down on the old market—a brujo spreads herbs and cures out on "his" section of sidewalk on a couple of pieces of sack and starts up business for the day—later my sister and I visit one of these cats looking for something to soothe Rachel's bowels, which Lucy has great revels in describing to old, withered-up witchman who looks like he shoulda took better care of himself in the first place—they always try to give you the piercing eye, those knowing ones.

I catch a familiar face down on the street, L's wife in a taxicab, L shouts, "Let's all go for a ride to my house, we been here all morning in this goddamn stinking mercado"—so I wrap up baby in some kind of clothes with hope enough of everything clean not to bring any righteous anger on my incapable head from good-doing Mexican mothers, or more likely spinsters who don't know what it's like anyway, and we drive, Mexicans, dogs, babies, children, and four exiled crazy people to the Villa Del M house of L, passing the whore mansion next to the beach which inspired everyone with awe not knowing what it's about—me, at least, to me it appears a very enigmatic setup, at night it has Christmas lights rigged up around the square roof which twinkles invitingly across the bay—I have never understood well the mystique of Veracruz whoredom, maybe Ray can tell me something about it.

I have no idea even what I talk about except that the picture comes to my eye and I just put down whatever goes down ... funny. ...

I must be excused for my emotional outbursts—it is invariably my errors catching up with me—by this time we had rented a house on Calle Revillagigedo—yellow stucco in the hot afternoon sun—three barred windows onto the sidewalk, the roof overhangs, yellow stucco inside too, shutters to keep out the rain, were they glass closing windows? I guess—the impression on moving into one of these houses is of stony bareness, the kitchen supports a cement sink—one in the patio, too, for laundry, a toilet, and shower, all the conveniences one could expect, tile floors—twenty dollars a month is very cheap, but we later found everyone else in our block of houses was paying ten and we don't even imagine where the following month's loot is gonna come from—the first a gift from L.

We had spent a couple of weeks in Mocambo, the real beach at Veracruz, ten miles out of town by a bus that left from in front of the post office where an *Hielo* man did a great business selling ices of papaya, piña, fresas, and many alternating weird melons, delicacies of the hot sidewalk around noon, waiting for the bus to take off to Mocambo, everyone packed in with all their market bundles, and what seats are not taken you can anticipate being broken—we start off finally, pass the Perroquia and the main hotel, pass another hotel near the railroad tracks I remember we stayed in one other time but not much sleeping in fact for the bus and trolley traffic just outside, making a turn and accelerating, kept waking us up, except for two or three quiet hours at night. We pass Villa Del Mar in the Mocambo bus, thank goodness for shades, the sun of ocean reflection on stucco seaside buildings is blinding, the dance hall on the beach is being scrubbed, both of them, too early yet for afternoon beer drinkers.

TROIA

We pass all signs of civilization now, making it through the scrub on a paved road heading further down the coast south of Veracruz, but we get off at Mocambo, scene of the Mocambo hotel resembling something on the Riviera—I am later to swim there nude in their archway-surrounded pool, while some waiter awaits us coming back for after-dinner coffee, my friend doing weird things in the water underneath me; I am always being overcome at the humor of situations unknown to any customers, for I shyly keep a straight face. Mocambo is just a small group of summer houses of rich people, only a few poverty homes in the immediate town, and a gas station back from the water far enough not to see on the highway where we often go for coffee and pan. Ray and me, as much as I enjoy the good food I ate while I was on a date (I am going to have trouble with how to call this hustling, usually I say "go out and get some money," try to be discreet and not mention the sex, or any love-coincidental relation in terming it for that would be too hard on our marriage; now what will I call it, dislike the term "john," guess I am not blasé enough, call them by name, but I can't remember) I always like eating cake and coffee with Ray best—but at Mocambo, the thing is to drink beer and eat shrimps if you have the money—but we had little money and were at this time to be housed for two weeks in the summer beach house of an eccentric painter who had left his servants in charge—we were to furnish them with fifty pesos a week to buy food, which we tried to do, and the chick turned us on to Mexican cooking, actually we bought maybe one chicken a week and lots of rice and beans which do us, and all little delicacies for her and her husband—this is what L told us, I found the food very good and don't see how she could have made it stretch so far as to cheat on us besides, but this is the story in

Mexico, most Americans I think do not ever comprehend how they live so cheaply—later, J, my Veracruz mama, will turn me on to the comforts of life.

But we had a bed here and sufficient to eat and us together alone for a while—the baby with L's entourage—they had begged to be allowed to take care of her, a thing I could not understand yet—they worshipped her because she was so white—we got her back after a couple of days with all kinds of instructions to take her to a surgeon right away for she was definitely twisted in one foot—we considered this all a myth, but started digging her movements and worrying about it, never to end.

We would not have been allowed to stay at Mocambo as long as we did except for the return of Rachel—as much of a problem as feeding her was, and the main reason for me going on the streets, Rachel was one of the keys to our survival in this destitute period—everyone loved her and all we had to say, or not say, to our hosts was, what will happen to the baby—and we were allowed to stay. On the beach one afternoon with a storm coming up and the wind blowing sand in our faces, I was sitting on a log, breaking the news to Ray about N. My conscience has never been strong enough to hold back from him secrets of this kind, though I usually wait till what I think would be a cool time to break the news. We would be talking about our sexual experiences to each other and I start to accuse him of things I suspect he has been doing in all his absences from me, and end up telling him of this thing with N. I was called a pig—a thing I well believed by the time this argument was through and I did not remain sitting upright on the log very long. Whew, that cleared the air—after that point it was fully believed that I was capable of walking the streets. I began to know what was expected of me. This was one of the few times in our marriage I was not forgiven.

And so that sets the scene. I have been a little too lyrical in parts perhaps, but it was not at all for fun or experience that I was forced to be a con artist—pure necessity sent me into town to try my luck, and that's what I have all along considered it, and don't forget in my head also that we are fugitives and I expect surely every time I pass one of the hip Veracruz cops that the end was truly in sight and it was, if I could have seen it, but that is later.

I even remember what I wore the first time I went out—pitiful, I guess, I had only a very short corduroy skirt I had purchased at a bargain store in Hoboken and it was no bargain—and a gift from one of our neighbors nearby, who it seems to me were conspiring for me to go out and get some money, too, a blouse of limp rayon which hung very low on straps that wouldn't hold so that sometimes it wasn't even hanging—what a farce that whole evening was—of course, there was the afternoon headache, trying to get out of it, and pleading with Ray, who answers me reasonably with our broke and hungry situation—so I go, walk, how did I make it through the streets with my shame and everyone staring at my outrageous outfit? I walk to the plaza, where not even having money for a cup of coffee, I sit in the park and feel miserable. I didn't even know how to come on; a little later I guess it began to shine from my face, but this was just an opener, some little punk sympathizes with me, admired me, and I talk him into coming home with me; Ray has insisted that I must bring someone home, he promises me 100 pesos tomorrow, mauls and kisses me on the way, my new outfit summoning open caresses on the street, heifer to the slaughter, I persuade Ray that he is to be trusted for the money, our little house certainly looks poverty-struck in the candlelight. Ray watching from the patio, I am sick. . . .

I should write this like a résumé so that I could get a job here in New York—things are not so different now. I joke about it, even then there was a kind of exhilarating joke about it when I was able to get money and even the horror of being the breadwinner dulled somewhat. But truthfully, it was only necessary in Mexico, and there unavoidable; here in New York everyone understands that when you get down to the bottom, you go without cigarettes, you eat at the Salvation Army, friends help you, though grudgingly, you don't even want to ask them, but they are there anyway. In Mexico, it was nothing but me and the general public between us and starvation and the jailhouse.

The first experience almost finished me, the circumstances, Ray watching, the fact that the little punk never delivered the money, and no doubt spread the news to all of his friends about me. From then on I felt hunted, furtive.

If you could see us now, eating bread and tomatoes every day and considering it even a treat to get enough of that. Ray goes for tortillas which I cannot stomach yet, and some lucky mornings maybe N has laid a few pesos on Ray. I go beyond the grocery store into the courtyard where there is a line long as at the unemployment office waiting to buy *gordas, tortillas* fried big and fat with black beans inside. They are truly delectable with coffee. Ray and I fight over them like mongrel dogs on the street, and little baby Rach digs them and is seen gumming a piece hungrily—poor baby got as skinny as we did almost, pitiful to see, and no wonder the willingness of our neighbors to offer us food, though we refuse it, feeling silly; maybe they were just being nice, it was hard for us to tell speaking so little Spanish. Little Mexican chicks knock on our door with plates of some kind of tortilla concoction with tomatoes and onions, they all have different names, depending on how they are cooked, *panuchos* and *gordas* were the best though. Ray was fascinated at the men who, come evening coolness, get out their charcoal stoves and begin to prepare *panuchos*, breaking up the chicken, chopping up lots of onion with a good soupy sticky bean paste and green tomato hot sauce and when someone comes in to eat they turn up the stove hotter and begin to cook them individually with a dash that suggests a French chafing dish artist.

The second day I either balked completely or Ray figured I was not able to pull a good enough con; probably both, and Ray went off to the center of town, El Centro, armed with a picture of me in a bikini, while I sat at home waiting nervously. I do not file my fingernails or such, but try to make the baby comfortable and hope that there will be no one outside the house when Ray comes home with his catch. And wow, my smart husband, did you come home with the drunkest man in town, figuring that is the coolest? How did you catch him? I am as curious about that scene as you are about all of my innumerable ones. He was a fat one, out drinking with his friend, two too-much cats, nowhere, afraid to have Ray around, figured he could bully me, talked Ray down to 150 pesos, which I make up for later copping fifty out of his drunken stupor wallet to pay for Ray's distinguished services, nearing dawn I put him together and shove him out the door, anticipating Ray getting back soon and our glee . . . hehehe. . . . Oh, he really did dig me, Ray, he wanted to do it twice, but I wouldn't let him. . . . (Is that me prostrate on the bed? Me handling all of that bulk to be serviced? I let myself get to a point where I put on a good show, forcing them to come and have done? ... Often having to put up with bullshit conversation ... Get on with it, Bonnie, you are a member of the great club and must grow to like it. ...)

It is morning now on Calle Revillagigedo and though the whole of Veracruz is awake, on the move, we in our house emerge into our own self-made world. Rachel would get up earliest of us three, I would wake to her gurgling goos in the crib alongside of us. I pick her up out of her nighttime prison-crib-bars and sit her in the little orangewood chair with green linoleum oilcloth seat with hole in it, facing the stucco wall, she sits looking at the picture gallery we have made for her out of classical paintings collected from Classicos matchboxes. She sits there for an hour continuing her contemplation while I return to sleep, next to Ray, oh sweetness of his hand touching my head now, the sun softly rising behind the clouds.

We found peace in Veracruz and became used to the hustle, and comfortable in our house. Free, I want to go back, we all want to go back. Now ... at this moment I want to be there, but time drags, and fate has done its demolition.

I watch the dawn come slowly, lying in the bed with Ray, begging him to let me stay, but we both knew that I had to go, and immediately, while I still had the bus fare. I left that morning, oh lonely, and the next day as Ray was painting pictures on the floor, the Mexican immigration people came and took him to the Veracruz jail, and when I got back from Mexico City a week or ten days later he was gone and the pictures were on the floor unfinished, the house was dusty and unaired, uninhabited. A letter under the door was from Ray, the first letter we ever received by regular mail, postmarked the 17th of August 1961, from Laredo, Texas.

TROIA

Man on the street, I spit in your face, just as I spat on the American Consul's doorstep with the information to him that his wife was a whore. He said to me, "we have heard for quite a while of your activities here in Veracruz, and your husband had stuck out like a sore thumb, too." I said, "we don't stick out like a sore thumb like you do," and he tried to keep me there by his authoritative tone, but I was far far beyond that and split out of there quickly—picked up the baby Rach from J and invited her to come with me to Xalapa to see her friend. J went to get a taxi, and her husband, the current one, went to get a couple of bottles of beer for the ride. . . . But I left the baby behind with J; you see I thought it was the end of the world for me, and I had not been sure all along if I wanted Rachel to participate in that with me so I left her behind with J who would have made her a good mother anyway. I wish I could have left her there longer, but they wouldn't let me cross the border without her, so I had to retrace my steps. . . . No, this is all mixed. I took a taxi from Veracruz to Mexico City; the taxicab driver brought his wife along so that they could have a "holiday." It cost me all of my money just to get away from Veracruz, for the immigration people were going to arrest me because of my papers.

I arrived in Mexcity from crossing the plateau of Puebla country in the morning redness and saw a whole nightmare of red individual mounds rising from the otherwise-level black silhouette as I try to sleep in the back seat, anticipating a busy day, and write a letter to Ray from Roger B's house all full of nighttime love and blues and fear of the end of all this; he interpreted this as a suicide letter and got as scared as I had at his. But it wasn't the end; it was just a very difficult and frightening interval as this is right now as I write this with Ray in prison. But I will tell it, tell it complete with no end or beginning, I am getting nervous with the immensity of it again. But I want to be alive, want to preserve my dream. This daily seeking has an end in my head so CAPITALIZE it. The revolution is starting tomorrow as I can start a revolution any time I like in my head. . . . I am getting too far out again, but that is nothing new.

It was not long before I was introduced to a Leading Citizen of Veracruz. One evening I was approached at the Perroquia by someone who wanted to take me to him and I did meet him in person, unbelieving. Anyway, knowing that he knew, I threw all caution aside and treated him like anyone else. There was nothing else to do, I guess. I never really possessed a hard enough hustle to handle him properly and trouble was to come of this, as he was not a kindhearted man. I found most men I fucked not sympathetic towards the existence of a husband in the picture, but I did not take the time to analyze this—just ignored it. Maybe I could have prevented a lot of trouble if I had analyzed it.

A drive up to his deserted street, where despite the dark night he is cautious and wants me to get into the house without being seen by his neighbors. He fucks me surreptitiously, meanwhile showing me his furniture, kisses me in a way I don't enjoy, fucks me timidly, and then wants me to profess how much I enjoyed it, hanging over the edge of his sofa. "Put it in quick;" he is not even interested in removing my clothes but is not possessed with the urgency that usually accompanies that symptom. I surmise that he is just plain in a hurry to get it over with. In time, I discover that I have presented a status challenge to him and I am surprised as I had not known how my reputation had flourished in such a short time. He talks of his mother. We could possibly be friends just by the virtue of his somehow twisted admiration of me (I had premonitions that there would be trouble from this relationship and I am sure to this day that he was involved in Ray's arrest) and in later times when I see him and he is not able to pay I visit his office at headquarters and he lays bread on me in installments. I saw my friend J there the first time. I walk to the desk and ask for Leading Citizen, she asks my name and business and I decline to answer either, but the eye of the Leading Citizen is caught and J reaches in her desk, face wreathed with fat friendly smiles, and hands me an envelope with the bread complete, a happy moment for both of us. J came to admire me from that moment and I later knew her worth, my dearest woman friend in the world maybe, J; although I got along well with all the madams, J, a dear friend and essence of Veracruz, was able to open up a well of social enjoyment and faith in myself I hadn't known before.

It is well into late spring now, probably June, Ray has gone to the post office and the baby is being taken care of by someone—I am expecting the Citizen's assistant—fat jive, friendly to me and Ray, he likes Ray so I am well disposed to be kind of casual friends with him. Besides he has promised the night before on his drop-by trip (he didn't have any money at the time) to bring some pot. Our record player is functioning again and I, in possession of seven pesos, have gone out in the hot sun to a wine shop a couple of blocks away in an estranged tree-hidden house with baroque bars made of wood shadowing the darkness of the shop which says that it is closed. Now my desire is increased for a bottle of wine and I finally succeed in buying a bottle. As I return home, the jukebox in the *refrescos* joint across the street has warmed up and will play maybe the same song for the rest of the day and far into the night, but it is a new selection today for I am not bugged, but start in on the wine, sitting alone at the wooden table contemplating. I like to sit by myself; I like to anticipate visitors. He arrives soon, black and hot already, happy and anxious, friendly, and opens up a piece of newspaper bundle under his arm (everything purchasable in Veracruz is likely to be wrapped with skill in newspaper) to exhibit an arm's thickness of stuff which we will be putting to the test soon. He also has 50 pesos to lay on me and I am pleased with the deal, having had enough wine in the early morning heat not to mind at all anyway. We tussle on the bed mattress on the floor ignoring noises from the outside for a while and are inundated in sweat of the sunny morning. Is this not God's honest clean sweaty labor and pleasure of good wholesome things? He sticks around long enough to greet Ray from the post office and that is that....

J's garden in the morning jasmine sunshine, or the evening clean clothes cool, she rubs jasmine flowers behind my ears. Her mother serves us black coffee, black beans, tortillas well baked—you never know what a feast of pleasure eating can be till you have accustomed yourself to this black Veracruz food. J and I speak intuitively, neither of us understands the other's spoken idiom, we speak gibberish which neither answers comprehendingly, but just talk because it is expected, yet we are dear friends, my jasmine fat sister, *yo te quiero jova*, I blurt with tears in my eyes, in my friendship with J. The policewoman procuress, P de la P was her actual title, which cracked me up, broke up all the American inhibitions I ever possessed; I know that I am as much Mexican as I am New Yorker or even spade, Negro, Veracruzana, I have undergone the metamorphosis completely and my heart is warm and happy. Whatever problem I have, J understands and miraculously produces the solution. Now that is friendship: every time I go to her house a burden is lifted from my shoulders. Though I was suspicious of her motives at first, and turned down her first efforts on my behalf and thwarted her plans at last by going to Mexico City, she even understood our need for occasional extravagance and did dig us, no question. I could write her a letter right now in English or in Spanish and she would be thrilled, happy to hear from me as if none of her present life had put any distance between us and I were there in her heart still. This is not mush: how many people can boast of such a friend as the three of us had in J? I will never suspect her of turning Ray in, though she was the Citizen's secretary. She warned me against him, she helped me to escape—but J, J, why did you call in the witch? Why the burning of offal in the baby's sweet presence? Why?

Or, flash ahead to Coatzacoalcos, a strain of pure music floats over the chilly breeze, we are both sunburned and have been writing human hieroglyphs of bodily dance on the beach the whole day. During the late afternoon in the seafood pavilion on the water, we eat soup and, chilly with the wind of unrelenting ocean, we realize the frightful power of the sea. We do not even go in the water, for its monstrous power is evident up to the even apparently gentle sea foam. Ray rediscovers the ninth wave, I try to draw the water but become overawed—we spy shark fins and backs wallowing at leisure in the port, going in and out to sea, marking the channel—woe poem, the sea foam.

Bad music most always has a violent effect on Ray—I am revolted at all the bad excesses of the freedom of direction the general populace with its taste will like, music that has bad meaning, bad spirit, and above all, bad sound. The jukebox across the street beats out the same song all day: "I haven't slept for three months, it's been three months since you've been gone, when will you come back"—a piano riff with cocktail clink piano.

All day my mind shrinks from the undesirability of what I have to do at night. In the morning I try to get things straight, afternoon somehow goes by in spite of a headache, with six o'clock approaching, I have to take a bath, and try to get as straight as no clothes will allow, nothing to stay for, but less than nothing to go for, yet I argue always to stay. We have big fights in the afternoon because of this. I am always trying to arrange some compromise. Fighting is better than nothing (I will later change my mind on this point) and I am finally mustered out of the house. I take a bus and try to lose my mind in the passing scenery, try to forget the presence of people and walk through the central parts of town quickly thinking, "fuck 'em, if they want me they can come after me, but they better be fast, and what's more, attractive." I am approached by unsuitable characters whom I ignore; there it happened, now I am truly justified in being furious, the creeps—I walk to the portside seawall to get away from it. The stepping-off point of blackness into the sea—I am running out of cigarettes anyway and walk back into the plaza area. Someone invites me to coffee; he is short, fat, dark, squat, charming (fifteen watt), and I go with him to sailors' seafood bar, drink too much beer and eat shrimps; he invites other people to the table and makes me kiss him in front of them, I comply with relish, my only choice—very late we go to his hotel, The B. He threatens me with no pay when I balk at a certain stage, I start to leave, he insults me, I get mad, he grabs me, I try to get away but am afraid to scream, he sees that I am about to scream, he grabs his belt and sits on the bed watching me while

I get dressed, too excited to think of what to do to him to make up for what I have been through, not to speak of the effort I have gone through on his behalf. He grabs my wrists and hits me a couple of times on my arms before I am able to get away. I fly frightened home, knowing that he will cause trouble. Ray hears my story, gets a knife from the kitchen, and goes downtown to find him; I spend the time in fear, wanting to be with Ray, and ashamed of having allowed such a scene to occur. Ray comes back later, unsuccessful, questions me further, and the incident ends there. But even if I had come back with money I would have gone out again the next day—so it was only another day, a bad one, I tell myself that this is a tough business, and should have expected as much.

Play me a danzón-flute lighted thump the Indian heart trip light across the snake-veiled dance floor. An Indian whore, her hair braided with ribbons and runs in her stockings, red shoes—the taxicab driver loves her—she only costs five pesos.

But I am getting ahead of my story and run the risk of telling various endings first and never getting back to the middle, leaving it like that. Excuse my timeless sentences, I want to experience it all over again, so take it on me to flash back again as necessary.

We were in Veracruz about six months; the season progressed from Del Nortes season into flashing hot summertime. Get smart and start walking on the shady side of the street out of respect for Van Gogh's madness, the same, the sun so desperately violent in mornings that you do not even realize what is happening to you until it is done. Ray goes to the post office a couple of times and by mistake lets the morning sun soothe away the aches of a chilly night, comes back to the house with a headache; like too much to eat, it is O.K. until you got it. So, sneak along the shady side and hurry to get back before the whole street is exposed.

I hang out just about every night, suffering not too many extremes and an occasional piece of good luck. During the day a chick across the street from our house allows me to use her sewing machine and iron, so I make it over there every afternoon with something in mind and slowly succeed in producing a standard imitation of the Veracruz girls' evening crispness, with a good part of my brazenness not excluded. I figure this will make things easier for me to look what I am and then I do not eternally have to get hung in explaining to people who might mistake me for a tourist.

My suntan is getting very fine and voluptuous which is a help also—Ray says I look melon-colored.

We continue to live modestly—a period of time when plums are in season—*ciruelas*, we are saved from bread and tomatoes, starting to eat fruits instead. I long for apples, a hopeless wondering about the future that, no apples here in Veracruz that I have seen.

I begin to suffer an apathy of inactivity at home—bugged that Ray and I never have any fun anymore, so the next time I score some bread we are all promised a trip to Mocambo. I think it would be fun to take the baby for a change, want to pass by the Palmas dancehall where Ray and I dance to the song "La Boa." Long nights of beer and cheese sandwiches to wash down the *mota, mi corazón, es para ti, todo los persones, ja saben ja saben,* oh dance that Veracruz swing, the heart wringing the sweetness out of every moment, Las Palmas.

Damn the pain; it must be written. Damn reality that all the present infections have to be drained from a stopped hole. Damn the metaphors and the scariness; it is the fever taking over.

Rise to me, visions of Mocambo. Hiss, lizards in deserted house yards by the beach, bleached logs I incarnate with spirits of lost Argonauts, here? In Mocambo? And why not, I say—does not the present moment bug me as if all eternity's infernal history staggered on its execution? So there—lizards, dragons, in fact, on that beach in Veracruz, come to eat us. We wander, the sand is too hot to allow for comfortable movement. Having money, we sit on rented chairs, I keep my eye on passersby, always extra susceptible to a little easy money, always waiting for luck to indeed intercede, damn the poverty said so often. I have even come to think that poverty is not meant for us and when we are poor it is bad luck and not just the regular schedule of things. Ray likewise looks at women on the beach, but I know that I have all the hustle at this point and he is just looking to get laid, don't ask me how I know, but it is true—oh fever fever deliver me from this clairvoyance! This is slop—I cannot remember—this is a composed interlude to what I knew happened at the time—does anyone blame me for embellishing the facts—be humble, Bonnie—the fact is I cannot remember if it was really Mocambo and the lizards hissed that day, or Villa Del Mar and faggots wrestling in their sandy suntans—I see me at the water's edge having just emerged from a dip, I am conscious of my thinness in the bikini and that is something—I am probably the only girl on the beach in a bikini—I shake the water from my hands—my wedding ring flies into the sand and sea foam and I frantically pursue it, spontaneously crying—God, what an omen, what a loss.

Mexican faggots laugh as I cry—always the extremities of emotion. How I hate them. Strange that I hate the Mexican men so and dig their women with no reserve. My hate for them is often boundless, and probably a reaction to not knowing metaphysically who is actually being took more, them or me.

I don my clothes on the beach; I feel so much contempt for the faggots and beach-dwellers who will not admit that I am even a little attractive, that I put my clothes on right there, not caring, or better, trying to bug them with my confidence. It doesn't worry me much anymore. Anyway after having shown everything, what is the shame in covering it up again?

Back to town now and the streetcar is cool after the steadily-growing-hotter beach sun. Photos of that day open my eye further to the happenings on the beach. Rachel and I sit in a beach chair smiling at each other's smiles, growing smilier with smiling. Who says we weren't happy? Later in the sidewalk cafe of the Hotel D we dig each other happy over ice cream sodas, Ray is wearing white trousers and a blue shirt with tails out and tucks and puckers in the front of it, he does not look jive like a Mexican, though dressed as they do, he looks like a movie star, and I, no doubt, too, in the skirt with slits up the side that I have premeditatively fashioned to entice eyes, the tightness of it shows the bikini I wear underneath, still wet and full of sand. I am constantly in a state of sensuality, my favorite condition. Baby Rachel still wears knit shirts and rubber pants salvaged from Hoboken, we have not yet discovered baby frills of Mexico, but soon, soon we will be completely initiated. The coolness of a garden fountain, the Hotel D sidewalk sitting-place digging people who go by and crazy buses lazy trolley cars, we sit for a long time, the ice cream soda and countless cigarettes. A man sitting nearby winks at me, I take it in its course, ignoring him (even if the family had not been with me I would ignore it for I require a total come on, proud) take no notice of him. We split. Ray goes to the post office probably, or maybe by this time he is friends with M, down next to the beach, or goes to see N and B afterwards, I am not hurt this time, there are things to take care of with baby Rach, besides this afternoon might be spent in making me a new dress to wow them with—anyway, somehow I walk complacently up the street, onto the streetcar. I do not lift my eyes at passersby the whole trip home, my mind on the afternoon and morning happy together on the beach, the sun still soothing me, though the Zaragosa trolley sweats up whoredom streets and weedy unkempt ways that will never get straight before the sun is too hot to do anything about it anyway. Baby Rach flakes in my arms, we pass the police station, I do not look, better to be seen and not see, people brush by me on the trolley, I do not look, but feel eyes boring into my back, why not, I look good enough, a fat boy on the trolley has alternating fits of graciousness and Johnny-fat-ass mischief, plays as if he is the back-of-the-trolley conductor, he bows at my exit, I anticipate having to slug him for some indignity but it doesn't come and I am relieved, off the trolley. I walk up the street, the baby is a sweet sleeping burden, totally flaked in my arms, face full of sleep. Someone is walking behind me; no, someone is walking beside me; someone is speaking to me. I do not look, unreasonably furious that the drunks would bother me so early in the day. I walk faster, and finally look up to show the contempt in my face; it is the man who winked at me and studied my face in the Cafe D. He has followed me all the way home, he says (I am insulted that anyone would have me figured in spite of all appearances against it—the baby in my arms!) he wants to take me out; I say no, emphatically, meaning it; he continues to walk with me. Then I decide to give him a try, he can come home with me and wait for my husband, then we will decide, oh sensuousness, oh easy con, who is conning whom?

The baby is put to sleep in another room and I sit in the canvas chair, overcome with the exertion of traveling all the way home, carrying her. He tells me I am very beautiful; he wants to spend the day with me and have some fun. He wants to take me out places, he is in from Mexico City on a holiday and wants me to keep him company—pitiful, weak come-on I figure—his name is A. I tell him I want 300 pesos figuring that that will end it or start an argument at least, but he agrees, that is not enough for me, I want the money there and then, but he would rather wait (honestly, that's what he said, and I have heard that line, so often, I do not believe) but I am still sitting in the chair, my sodden bikini shows through the dress. He is on top of me, rather under me working upward. I am the deity being worshipped, this is something I cannot cope with, my dress is pushed upward and then dispensed with—oh, hot afternoon—I know that I am better off without clothes, sandy legs being caressed, no manual labor this, I am completely relaxed, except an occasional thought of the unpocketed money causes me to tremor. My hands are on his head pushing him away, but he insists, head on—my morning in the sun has left me uncome anyway—so—we are soon together in the chair, in each other's laps, I rejoice at his uncomfortable position and make things even more uncomfortable for him, oh legs and thighs, sweat, sand, and saltwater we come—we are friends now and I want a cigarette.

Although exalted over him (how is this, have I swallowed his lie? How does fucking make people close? Was it fun to give it away for free?) I am in the position now of nagging him for the money; he tells me not to worry, that we are going out to have some fun; so I decide to follow him around and follow it up. I take a shower and put back on the same clothes as we are going to the beach. I leave Rachel, still asleep, at a neighbor's house. He has seen my poverty, also seen what it encompasses. Who could be richer than us, and I am determined to bug him with it; he apparently digs it and I figure maybe he is straight, but the worry does not leave my head. We do not wait for Ray, but make it. Late afternoon, I have had a shower with him in our little cool bathroom, and we go to drink beer at Villa Del Mar in the Bailando place with the sun setting almost, but still hot enough that I can swim, in front of his eyes, the more I am by myself the better—he watches me—I watch his watch—it is *cuatro in la tarde*—do I want to eat—no—the floor is shiny, people are looking at us—I disdain them—swim more and sit laughing at the pleasures of life, with him.

He has treated me all along very graciously—as if I were a queen—no doubt he says just that, *"mi reina,"* and I am flattered and contemptuous at the same time (I still do not have the money) we go back to the Hotel D, but I come up with a new one on the way "I have no underwear, how I am going to sit through dinner in a wet bathing suit—I have been wet all day"—we laugh and he buys me drawers in a women's dress shop; he asks if there is anything else that I need—I look around at the sumptuousness of the American shop wanting to try everything on, but suddenly shy—and end up with a horrible pair of pedal pushers (though American) and a knit tee shirt, and a pair of sandals. I probably look better in my old rags I think, but I am dry and elated over his generosity, also embarrassed to have him so call my bluff—the poverty bit—I allow myself to be taken into the fancy dining room of the hotel. I think with glee that I have never been there before. He orders with an extravagance I have never before enjoyed in Veracruz. We drink delicious red wine and I know that this is the way I should always be treated and began to feel truly queenly, waiting for some old acquaintance to see me, I am having fun! A friend of his appears—oh romanticism—a bullfighter, famous, I do not expect to be come on to by him, but he is polite, and I am at a loss for words, in spite of the wine, and the food, the food is no good, although very expensive. I do not eat, I am confused thinking it will soon be over and don't see any way to plan the end as things are completely out of my control.

I am taken to a hotel on the plaza. I delight in the view from the balcony and would show myself naked to the crowd, but he gets serious again, "*mi reina*," fortunately I am drunk and so things proceed. Black night comes up the stairs over the wooden bannisters; half twilight shows from the sky over the wooden bannistered balcony. The promenade has been started in plaza's dance—fresh clothes and fresh ideas, everyone has just awakened from the afternoon's sensuality and noises grow with the lights, looking everywhere to get laid, apparently. I am prone on the bed caught in my own snares—big daddy (no, little daddy in this case) wants to do well by me, instructs me to relax on the bed while he goes over me, wants to bring it all out it is apparent—he is beside me feeling my drunkenness in every direction, no more mutual contact at first than a reassuring kiss, then I am to be aroused, I am felt and played with, tantalized, my movements do not yet betray what I am thinking as I try to keep still, it is not right that I should give in so quick or easy, stem the flood rising, he goes down on me finally and I give way, the true me comes out and

TROIA

we are in it, fucking uncontrollably. I outdo myself and in the end it is drawn between us excelling the other—then having let go too much of what I am, I am called upon (surely discreetly) to go down on him, guess what is beckoning, I am ready to stop and leave at this point, but what I am being paid for after all, 300 pesos is enough and I have certainly been courted, besides in fucking I guess I always give away my true nature, once having let go completely I am somewhat ashamed at enjoying what I am paid for, enjoying it immensely at times and when I don't I put on a good enough show so that none would ever know—I am able to close my eyes and dream of myself alone—so I do it, but not for long—he finds it unbearably pleasurable and we go to take a shower and I am allowed to go down on him in the shower—he hangs ecstatically from the shower knobs—then for a cool refreshed fuck, the last one obviously, he is exhausted, he sleeps while I clean up alone in the bathroom, then to his side, hoping fervently that he will go soon, I am quite completely ready to take my money and go—but there is no problem, he gets up, I am left to contemplate the balcony's nighttime in a sheet, he joins me on the balcony and waves to the bullfighter who is below waiting for him, I sigh relief in my heart—we are ready to go—before I say anything about money on the dark stair descending he hands me a bill, I think it is less than I asked taken aback by its singularity, but in the dim light I see it is 500 pesos, oboy, I am a success.

Music on the street, we drive in a car. Music in the car, I am being sung to. My shyness has returned and I feel in an awkward position. I am given his address in Mexico City and am urged to visit him and I agree; he sings to me and I am pleased with him enough to be enchanted by his voice. Who is conning whom, finally? I ask leave to go, and I catch a taxicab home—ah, release—after all of that, the greatest pleasure is to go home with the bread. Ray is not at home, so I go to N's and find him there listening to records—exhausted in my new clothes I am questioned by B and N and I tell them simply that I met a guy on the street who bought me all new clothes. B turns green in spite of her disapproval, especially when it comes out that I have got 500 pesos to boot. If at anytime B was influenced towards vice, this was the moment, but she was to get back at me years later. Ray and I head home; Charley Mingus has twisted my tired-out head and Ray plies me with questions, not bad ones, considering the money in his pocket; it is still early, he goes downtown to look at this area that has become so enchanted for me. My price goes up and Mexcity looms. Lucy breezes in on a distinguished wind from Acapulco—her dress fresher even than Mexican fresh, her eye sharp from supervising the baking of tortillas. A super-deified headmistress, she always seems to me with her hair higher than any unbelievable hairdo I had imagined could exist. Her hair goes straight up in the air to a super self-made pyramid; her earrings are long and heavy and she tells me that her jewelry is pure gold and she wears it ostentatiously on the street, for all she is worth. She has grasped the essence of Spanish colonialism; unknowing, she flaunts it along with her hatred of Indians. I know immediately that we are enemies, even though so close in blood—Lucy who has always comforted me through a sense of duty. She picks up on the one thing of worth to her in the house and confiscates it—the baby. She tells me I am too thin; she is shocked by my thinness, chastises me for it; my hair has been dyed blonde for a long time and she tells me it looks awful. I can count on any member of my family to criticize me as close to my heart as they are able. She walks down the street admired as a cruel queen might be by the Mexicans and our friends. She starts talking to people in the neighborhood and I suspect her of completely straightening out any misunderstandings that might have been caused by our reticence mixed with unmasterful tongue. And yet I am close to her; in spite of all of it, I feel sorry for Lucy and always have; she has never known a love as I do and never will, incapable of it, and yet she lives her life; she is of course immediately a captive of my Rachel's existence, not her piercing judging eyes full of compassion, not that, but of the infant existence, and yet maybe Lucy knows something that I will never know, too, and cannot now even fathom; I do not want it, as she does not want my husband's love, but we have a common love between us at this particular time—the baby. She has brought her maid with her, as all good Spanish women would when traveling. She is married to a Mexican in Acapulco who will later break her heart and her bankbook; I have stopped feeling sorry on those occasions, she has been married as many times as my father and is incorrigible, nothing new in this world, people don't change. She invites me to Acapulco—so I return with her across plains and mountains, rivers, Mexico City Metropolis (where I try to hustle a professor at the U of Mexico, who wants me to be his mistress but won't even give me cab fare home, the late late night escape away from under winding lanes of live oak trees and my heart breaks wanting Ray). It has been hard for the baby Rachel up to this time and I would like for her to get healthy and also allow me some respite from care of her to become what is necessary. I embrace my prostitution. In Acapulco, the house is high on a hill, overflowing balconies of pseudo-back-to-nature, so this is what a resort is like. Get just close enough to grab up what you want of nature and then stick your thumb in its eye—I do not like Acapulco—I go walking at dawn knowing that the Indians must live somewhere and I find them though the way is tortured and hidden on secret hillside entrances. I walk up gutters of rain flow from impoverished backyards over someone living above to another chicken-coop up higher—a troop of little boys follows me—the gringa is better known here than any other city in the country—I feel a great compassion and want to live in one of those hillside houses of wicker branches propping someone precariously on his neighbor—and once or twice I see a house so ghettoed and isolated that it would be like a Chinese puzzle to gain entrance. I delight in glee in the Indians all around in the hill—ha! they have us surrounded—give it back to yourselves Indians! It is as easy as that—how I hate the American Spanish.

"A hotel on Mario Molina," is that the B? Veracruz again, send up your order of streets to vision anew my story, fill in these last few details before it is all done and squarely accounted for; no need to tell the rest of Acapulco, anyone who has ever been to Acapulco knows the rest and, if not, the travel folders on Third Avenue are adequate enough information, reckless tourism. I leave quickly with tears in my eyes for the baby Rachel, I have given you over, down the dry quartz-ridden hill I walk to the bus stop with tears in my eyes, looking back over my shoulder at the cruel queen, till I am past view and driving through coconut plantations. Quickly now Veracruz, reach out and rescue me . . . Lucy had moved to the B at our suggestion, for we had stayed there in our hotel days, making three separate episodes at the B, and the front rooms were really nice with clean, flowered curtains blowing out in afternoon naps, the front rooms on the street—the room to which the nut had taken me was one of the upper inner rooms with no escape, where I had beaten him with a belt (in clearing up past dubious mistakes, I will leave it hanging, like judgment in New Jersey, let someone else toss a coin which way it might have been. Who will say it was I or he that did the beating—self-defense is a byword in Mexico anyway, expected to be successful, if someone doesn't defend himself from a murderous attack then he is to blame for not doing so, so figure it all out for me someone—retain the stains as evidence, Veracruz—I await a clearer vision, being far past it all, fugitive now in life, though supposedly free). So Lucy was the third to stay at the B, and one day when I drop by to visit her the proprietor lets me into her room to wait, for she is out to breakfast—I relieve her of an unlucky charm, an opal ring, which I will not even try to defend. I have not always been a petty thief, and I put the ring to good use and did not even remember having borrowed it months later when she came back and saw it on my finger and said she had been wondering where it had disappeared to—and I returned it freely with no comment—although I could say I had saved her from some evil opal doom, taking the blame on myself. How much of this is true? I don't feel guilt anymore, not even for the worst of it. For isn't capitalism the big steal in reality? And anything I could even do would never counterbalance it. I would live a life of crime freely if it fit me, but this is only poetic justice I tamper with.

Isn't it funny how unemotional it all becomes if you tell the ending first, and then tell it again? Actually I have done no more than set it all up so that I can knock it down at my will. I am a great believer in self-determination, so if I sometimes seem flippant it is because I ascribe little importance anymore to external events for I am involved in the personal handling of them—these experiences, as my life, have heightened my abilities of calculation. I am like a gem appraiser and, like him, I see the worth of a truckload at a glance and it has always kept me close to Ray and Rachel in heart. Are we not three of a kind? I simply would like to spend my life in valuing the worth of an internal growing hardness.

I am full of moods and bad humors, always brooking my importance as the breadwinner. When revolutionaries come to stop at our house on their American way to Cuba, I am ungracious, not timid, but contemptuous. They are on their way to Cuba and idealism and here we are left to grope with the snake of time and capitalism growing; I wince every time I see a Coca-Cola sign.

Lucy returns in the jukebox afternoon; she has reconsidered, thinking that it might be better for her to doom the baby to our arms. She will no longer take care of her as she has been infected by my vice. Say that I am taught by my sister? She is five years older than I, but I can plant seeds of youth in the pit of her memories that torture her; she has come to Veracruz to try her luck! Ha! Small victory, that.

It is afternoon again on the beach at Mocambo. Rach, Lucy, and I and the maid and Lucy's Veracruz boyfriend who is to make more of a fool of her than my street walking ever showed me to be, for at least I have the pride of honesty and money in the pocket. She, Lucy, pretends to love him. Have I not said before that she can never love? The way I know it: she loves his money, but never gets more than a 1500 peso settlement which never comes through and she withstands the horror of a final huge burn and will never speak to him again, but does. Like puppy love she cannot see or tell where she is—oh well, I will comfort her; haven't I given her back her ring? Her hair grows higher in newly acquired tortoiseshell combs, she loves Veracruz way beyond pictures of tourism, her black soul embraces it; I grant you a black soul, Lucy, but I must not talk more this way. It is not right that I should curse my own blood. Thank the poets I have been saved from such a fate and better all my exile than to tempt that loveless life.

    I walk to the seashore with the baby Rach chewing on some discarded tail, her current favor, cut out for her pleasure from a mad hunting cap. We call a photographer to get her and me together as the side of the eastern sea wash over our feet and as he focuses a wave comes unexpectedly high to kiss her feet and gets her little pure cunt in a wash of foamy come, the diapers fall about her feet discarded and she looks at the cameraman with a grimace of double purity, picture of her infant womanhood, always pure my muse Rachel, I grin, she chews on her dog tail. Hang on, baby, to all that is sweet, the sea loves you and would forsake the turning of the whole world for your blessing. Diapers fall, it is all a big allegorical joke, I say. Our Sunday visits are spent in talking up details that will touch every nerve of desire that ever has been wakened before and during the week it builds. I dig out more information to satisfy him and have been confronted at every new piece of memory that has been buried and untouched for three years by a change in me, an awakening of that part of me that memory composed. And so as this story has grown I have grown. And what's more, the situation has grown around me, and I have shaped it with my eyes to take me more so back into other memories and as I shaped, it stayed that way. It has truly grown up around me. I say that everything I have written has become true, again, doubly true. I want to fuck, and not only that, but the manner in which I will fuck is becoming evident. So build more on it, keep writing; yesterday at the

MEXICAN MEMOIRS

Sunday visit with Ray I took him more news of the world as it truly is now. He has told me with no hesitation that I am a whore, emphatically, he loves my whoreness—so fuck!

So—as I increasingly pose the truth—what am I to do with it—this weekend I picked up a man on 42nd Street who could have supplied me with rent money that I need now, but I left him drift away. My eye is on visions of writing it instead. What is the truth and how far does it go? How can I erect the truth and then be twisted away from its undeniable presence?

This is the exact same situation of illusion. Is it understood now? The double life I am leading and the two parts yearning toward each other, I wonder, is everything about to fall? Ray tells me to fuck with as much sweetness as he did in Laredo when he was in jail there and I had no money, but didn't want to hustle with him locked up like that. He told me not to be afraid and that I must I take care of myself: "so go and get some money to do it," and I did.

Or should I say a triple life; there is the life of letters, too—those letters in Laredo between us: courage, hope, and a dawning of poetry, too.

I started writing to Ray when I went to Mexico City to pick up money for rent and taking care of the baby et cetera, not knowing that Ray was being busted at the same time and probably in Laredo already. These letters chronicled my gains in that period of a week, so get back into it—write those letters again here to explain the confusing transition from Veracruz to Laredo, via Mexcity, my head meanwhile tearing apart. . . .

TROIA

Letter addressed to Ray in Veracruz:

Dear Ray—   Monday morning.

Got 500 and some as of last night—hard working cause started out so low and have to fight the rats for every cent but haven't been burned—contemplated sending rent money so the landlord won't bug you but decided there isn't a safe way—but I will start back tomorrow with enough to cover our debts if nothing goes wrong.

Enclosing 50 for you to eat and the baby.

Spend all my time on the streets except to sleep a little—so lonely for you but the growing stash brings us closer together and soon we'll have us a fiesta in Veracruz, you and I.

                                                                          Love, Bonnie

Ray—   Tuesday

I'm so disappointed and lonely and worried about you and the baby—as I write this I have 425 pesos and haven't paid the hotel for three days. As soon as I score again I will send this and the rent money but I want to send 500 cause I know you are broke—I can hardly walk, my feet are raw from cruising all day every day. I haven't been taken but have had to fight like a wounded bitch a couple of times. Don't get many whistles even and it rains every day in the evening for three hours. Every time I think of you I choke up. I went into Bellas Artes and cried when I saw Sequeiros' paintings but didn't like the other stuff too much. Blew five pesos on a print but you'll like it. Hope this money cheers you up—I know you are as desperate as I and worried about me. I decided last night that I have to stay here as long as it takes to straighten us out and so I will send you sums as I get them because it's not coming fast enough to save the whole amount—the 400 is in the Hotel safe now and I am in a cafe near Insurgentes cause it's raining again. I am staying out now till I score; nothing to go back for, but soon as I score I will pick up the 500 and register this to you. I thought I would be back today at the latest but only Lady Luck knows what's happening now. My hours are full of fear and loneliness without you. I'm going to write the telephone number here when I get back to the Hotel. Call me collect if something happens.

Love, Bonnie

next day.

I wrote a letter to Bee last night and asked her for 50; she should come through soon. Didn't score yesterday although I walked for 12 hours; just went to see A and got 50 to fuck on his office floor. He says he will fuck me for 500 tomorrow so I wait and come home tomorrow night. I am going to beat the N Hotel; I owe them 125 I guess. Tonight at six I saw the coach for 200. Luck seems to be picking up. So lonesome for you; I am mailing all I have now, use it as you think is best but try to pay 400 rent if possible cause I will send or bring more immediately and M is also due here yesterday and will lend us some.

Love, Bonnie

I think that this is the last letter Ray got in Veracruz; I see the hotel as I write. I had taken along a de Sade book and read a little of it before sleep each night; it is *Juliette*, a story of a whore, like me. Not resting much, I see a quick flight into the bathroom to get myself straight and on my way out to the streets, determined, with necessity pushing me, but the thunderstorm every afternoon seemed to stand between me and my return to Veracruz. This was the beginning of my really hard hustle. I would not rest on my honors of having picked up some money but continued to worry about the total sum and the loneliness it was going to deliver me from. These letters to Ray had worked up to an astonishing disappointment when I got back to Veracruz finally. Ominously I had said "call me if anything happens. . . ."

Telephone number at the Hotel N: 22-68-90 (Rm. 206)

Dear Ray—   *Thurs. morn.*

I hope you got the other letters O.K. and the money—I sent them all together in a brown envelope—I didn't count the money but it was about 420 pesos. I am enclosing the registered slip—in case you haven't gotten it yet take the slip to the P.O. and make a big stink.

I just got 100 for fucking O last night, but afterwards he took me to a nice whorehouse to see if I could make some money there cause my feet were too raw and bloody to walk the streets. There weren't any men there, but a real nice chick saw me and said she had a rich friend she could call who would dig me and pay well so she called him but he works in his office on Thursday so he said for her to tell me that he would pay my expenses if I would stay two more days. He called me this morning at the Hotel and I am going to his office to talk at 12:30. If it's O.K. and looks profitable I will stay till tomorrow night. Also after that the coach took me to a party at his niece's house where there were supposed to be a lot of rich doctors, but they were very draggy so I left disgusted. Had trouble sleeping, so worried and homesick. You probably feel like I've deserted you and am having fun cause I'm such a jerk, but I just keep trying to straighten us out so I think I should stay. Tonight I see A for 500—with that and the 500 I ask from this cat I talked to this morning we should be completely in the clear. I'm going to send at least 50 with this. Try to pay the rent if you haven't. Haven't heard from M yet. I know you're bugged, baby, but be cool and wish me luck and maybe I will come home glorious.

Love, Bonnie

Come home glorious. I step into a taxicab, disembarked from the Veracruz ADO bus station. Hello, Veracruz, how relaxed the streets, it is late afternoon. The women and children are sprinkling the sidewalks and nearby to the houses are patches of bare ground, with water to keep down the dust. Veracruz creates its own coolness in an easy, domestic gesture; the afternoon becomes cool with drip drops of water from brown fingers, from hands browner than those in Mexcity and no one knows where I have been or how I came back. I see the Veracruz movie through happy eyes returning to Ray and the baby Rach, but there is a note of fear, too. I have received only one letter in all the long ten days I have been away. What has happened . . . ?

Have I told about O—Humberto O, the coach at The University, fat, plump with Falstaffian belly, therefore always good for a blow job.

In fact, I could otherwise not make it with him. He is always asking to turn on to pot also and hits on me for that shortly after he arrives in whatever hotel room I am stashed in. We talk of developments for a short time; there is never any interest lacking in my narratives, though sometimes the despair hits a little too hard, but, like J, O joyously approves our methods of survival and what's more, makes a great show of thinking me a good whore. O never lets me down that way, never cooled his commentaries with me over the whole six months or so that I knew him, whenever I called his house he was ready and anxious to do my bidding. He was not good for much bread, but he recognized the call of hunger or peril, et cetera, which is something. After we talked a little about these things we would maybe smoke a little roach; he would just taste it and I would inundate my head with it, cooling allowing myself to be as much in illusions' light as pot will allow. I usually received him into the room unclothed, in drawers, playing pin-up that way and we would smoke and he would sit next to me, totally undesirable, the old-time revolutionary. He related episodes to me of his times with Pancho Villa; about the time they all held up the train full of gringos to rob them and raise money for supplies for the revolution and fuck all the American women, who secretly loved it, as I can well imagine, and I enjoyed his stories and believed every word of them. I asked him of Sequeiros, being thoroughly turned on to his beauty after one viewing of his paintings at Bellas Artes, and I know that even native Mexico is down on this beautiful painter of the land, this true exposer of oppression. O told me that he has seen him in jail, in the federal prison near Mexico City and that he has a cousin there who works as a guard and that I could get in to see him if I wanted to. His hand was on my leg as we talked, rubbing me hard, pushing in between my thighs which were crossed, as intimate as my own hand would be. It knew exactly the pleasures that would most quickly get it there; he was a con that way. I can well imagine him talking with the young Swedish girls that he coached in swimming at the University. He would sit next to them in a restaurant and put his hand on their knees in such a friendly manner and would urge that they drink more—oh, bringing out the whore in them all, all those expatriates. He says to me to lay back on the bed that he is going to get me good and excited so that we can have a very good fuck. His English is not at all limited; so I lay back and he does not hesitate, taking off his clothes carefully. The overflow of his slack and dead flesh does not at all make him modest, since he is so rightfully proud of days gone by and has not given up yet at all, I cannot help but admire him at least as much as the situation requires—the old cocksucker—he straddles my head and shoulders and plants one on me, dangling his eensy cock imperiously for me to fondle. I play with him as if he were a woman, having found that is the quickest way with him and he teases me with his mouth pleasantly so that the pleasure and the pot go to my head simultaneously and every once and a while I am nudged by his drooping thigh to get busy on him also. His ass is so awful fat with old flesh drooping that I can feel the bones with flesh sacks hanging. I gag on his cock, but am not repelled knowing it is good old O. I come slightly and impatiently move my thighs inviting him to turn sport and do it. His limp cock becomes hard and we fuck and somehow my largeness contracts him into me miraculously and I put on a great show of fucking him mercilessly, making him come and he loves my attitude; it was just what he wanted.

Through Pilar, an old-time whore friend of his from way back, he introduces me to Emanuel de la G who summons me to his office. I wear my old raggedy voluptuous tight skirt with enormous slits up the side and my forever-blue furry French hat so I look the same nationality of whore-girl, bespoken poor. A has taught me the come on of that in Veracruz—poor whore, more elegant in nakedness, so dress accordingly. We interview over a Pall Mall, a prelude to riches to come, I know what he pays already. 800 pesos and from the way he talks about being busy at the office I know it will not be a long haul—it is decided—he makes a telephone call to a place he knows for the woman there to fix us up a room (another whorehouse! Mexcity abounds in them)—and we drive there in his distinguished black car in the hot Mexcity, *Zocalo* heat of open pavements and uncontrollable dust from the evaporated lakes—Cortez' biggest mistake, Mexcity is a nightmare of the dream it must have been of lakes and straight solid standing rock houses simple with the primal worshipping fervor; it has now become Spanish trash and dust and shame. Trystful, we have kissed in his office—me drawing him on with my poor-French elegance, him rebuffing me with his "Spanish" ancestry, divine right to run this sewing machine factory or whatever it is.

In the room—quiet and cool—the whorehouse business peaceful in the hot afternoon, not time yet to get busy to receive visitors, the room is quiet. I take off my clothes, I am bikini tanned; he takes off his and is surprisingly young and powerful beneath his pinched face; his lungs rising in his chest in a pride that seems more Indian to me than Spanish, though I say nothing. He has a hard-on already, a proud and youthful hard-on, we sidewise fuck going over it three times straight up and down sidewise in order to finally make his proud dong come. I am dismayed that he will not come and he grips me, not allowing

MEXICAN MEMOIRS

me to show any excess effort than just that straight up and down. Finally, condescendingly, the proud thing comes. I am almost surprised that he does not take it out at the final moment, but he has no sense of humor and takes it all very seriously—the only person I have ever met who exceeds me in these few things—I am in awe and decide not to like him.

Speaking afterwards he forgets condescension for a while and we talk of my husband and family back in Veracruz. I talk fast and full of feeling; having been away from them ten days now I am desperate to get back. No, I will not stay another day. He takes an interest in my family I think, because it has a lot to do with the illusion of poor whore I have created, embellished with the pride of being loved and I don't give a fuck for you or anyone because of it. I am perhaps a different kind of whore than he has mostly met; he tells me a little of his wife, whom he does not like, and his mistress who always tries to swindle him.

. . . . .

It was so hot that morning that I woke for the second time in the hotel—a patio out the window with shrubs—it looks to be unused, forever reflecting in every direction from the tiles, the hot sun-glazing heat with humidity already preparing the second thunderstorm in each of two days since I have been there—I wake with a headache and not much enthusiasm about anything and lonesome—I had probably awakened for a few moments at dawn but that was too excruciatingly lonely for me to abide—there was nothing facing me but hustling until the work was done and the rent and bills to be paid and nothing between me and the world of other people's existence than whatever façade I can erect on myself before it is time I go out the door, and God—today I am at a loss—one hopes only of an easy and fast score and I go to see A in his office.

I walk out of the hotel—it is god-hot and awful. I am immediately dejected—I walk without seeing past the markets of candy and clothes, the area swarms with flies and bustle of this and that going here and there so fast I get bugged with having to walk through it all—a good mile's walk through all of this ahead of me and no pleasure in my shoes. Still I do the best I can and try to keep my head up, knowing I am not creating much of a sensation in any manner.

A is friendly—he is cool and well-disposed behind his large desk in his private office—he sends his secretary out to lunch after we talk for a few minutes—I am hot and not especially interested, but desperate—the safety pins in my dress are going to bug me with the whole scene—on his lap we kiss—he senses my mood and somehow warms to it. Quickly my dress is around my waist and I am on the floor, safety pins exposed amongst the tatters—the carpet is suitable but not comfortable and I am close to tears as being fucked—Oh my soul, what a mean blue day—A gives me fifty pesos and says he will see me later when we can go out together and have some fun—I am not pleased at all by the incident and fun is certainly not my object. I am walked to the street and go discouraged by the bus back to my room to prepare for evening . . . I will not forget the shame of my arms around your neck on the floor there in that nice office when I needed your help, and you discouraged me—take 'em while they're proud and happy in Veracruz and put a twist on things, but now I rank you with the rest—things could have been worked out more kindly—but now I am free of you and on the straight hustle. Why was I so seldom afraid of violence—I am afraid for me backwards—or was I the scary one?

· · · · ·

Rumble coming—thunderstorm approaches in the Mexcity afternoon—tacos are selling like crazy—if I was a few months older, I would know of other places to make it in a thunderstorm-cool—*sopa de pescado* on Calle Dolores, with my hair in curlers till late afternoon—like everyone else—but myself still too at the same moment of being transformed in whatever photograph studio—that amazes me—but the thunder comes underground first—starting from the mercado, nearby welcome Cuauhtémoc booms over the truly perpendicular station of the market—the heart of Mexico bleeds in dust-shaded yellow walls awaiting the drip drop.

This is the last episode in Mexcity before I bus-trip back to Veracruz, the night I was to have fun with A and give him another chance. I have spent the afternoon in normal living; I have eaten eggs scrambled with beans in the Chinese restaurant below the Hotel N, and for dessert, strawberry cake and coffee in a glass. I have already picked up enough money to straighten everything out. Emanuel de la G was the supplier of the balance, but if I can get together another 500 out of A, Ray and I can have money to vacation for a few days in Veracruz together. I am relaxed.

Six o'clock tryst time in Mexcity—downstairs from A's office—Calle Santiago—around the corner is a cocktail lounge downstairs where I start off with wine—though my dress is not exceptional, I am so confident that my face is flushed with color, and the wine doesn't hurt. Let me look at it six or seven ways—I don't want to miss anything either.

The two others were sympathetic persons, who looked to be a little faggish, though not the skinny sort, the kind with receding hairlines and oh so gently elegant suggestion of ovals in all their bodily features, helped me through the evening, several times told the other two that they had bad manners, and when it came their turns to fuck asked me if I wanted to—fell in love with me and wanted to see me again—but at the crucial end of the evening when I could have known the truth about him, he passed out from extreme intoxication. The other was a blonde husky Canadian who spoke perfect Spanish being somehow also Mexcity bred—he comes on winking at me all the time behind the others' backs—the three of them and a fat dark mustached (probably government official) who declined to enlarge the party but met with us in the cocktail lounge around seven—I had only expected A of course, and the others, in fact, are talked into the party with successive drinks—no mention of money—surely A has told them; it is all clear, no doubt, but in this case I save being explicit in the last and lose several hundred pesos because of it.

Oh Mexcity time-snake, beast of the sidewalk cafe, let me go back to Veracruz where time stops. (I am already back in Veracruz and this is just an evening's game—funny sometimes, how I really fit into the picture.)

Suggestion of a thunderstorm and night makes a noiseless thunder in its sudden fall, the garden tinkles, someone's Volkswagen has been unparked from garage and directed and we have arrived too early for rain, too late for meaning, night has inexplicably come and arrived us at the scene of a large Sartrean coffeehouse called the Fifth World (El Lobo . . .). Shuddering horror I am questioned right to left as I have been the inspiration for this coffeehouse. I am in a blue French wooly beret of existential street-walk all the way from Hoboken to here. HOBOKEN, how you have changed! The storm alternates with night, I lose track. I am already fully drunk on brandy—let's get it over with, I cannot be induced to talk, this is not an interview.

I speak with A behind my hand and say that if this is not what I had expected it would be I had best be off already to Veracruz—he tries to shush me, making like he doesn't want to embarrass his friends with the expense and won't, don't I trust him for it—he is so drunk already, but I figure to chance it; I have been promised 200 pesos each. The temptation to risk it wins me over.

I don't know why I was so reluctant to talk the money over with all of them. I had never been involved in one of these gangbang scenes before and I was not the only one who was self-conscious. All the fun they intended to have was forcefully taken. The fat blonde Canadian tried to tease me about my occupation. The coffeehouse was full of young creeps of totally unenchanting type and we split there quickly though it is not late yet, and go by Volkswagen to the waiting house in Colonia. I admire the swimming pool and am invited to swim but not with enthusiasm, so I don't. I am ushered self-consciously to the waiting cot, next to a ping pong table and, as I said, laid in sequence by the three of them, the others carousing in adjoining long rooms of empty space, no sign of domesticity in this modern house of many picture windows, the tall dark guy trying to make like he loves me, and A his regular self. I am frantic with being treated so casually and not enjoyed, the tall dark guy fucks me twice making like he enjoyed it a great deal, and wants me not to continue with the others after I finish him. At least it was an attempt at appreciating me, and the fat Canadian disgusts me with his empty conception of up and down, athletic notions of making love and checks with me if I have had any disease even before he will venture in. If I were to arrange a gangbang myself it would not ever be this disgusting little boy play stuff. I am totally disgusted with the scene long before it ends; we all shower together and I do not talk; they drive me to the hotel where in the car before I get out I openly ask A for the 600 pesos, the tall dark one meanwhile asking my address in Veracruz. A pretends to be more drunk than he is and the others seem to not know what it is all about, thought I was just out for love, so I end up with 300. But I am glad to be rid of them. I sigh and bathe carefully in the hotel room, exhausted in spirit and so glad to be done with Mexcity and on my way back to Ray who can encourage me and console me, and my baby Rach. I am finally going back to Veracruz.

So goodbye, Veracruz, I take my farewell. Your carnival sun and banshees of superstition awoken in nighttime gutter-streets of passing by give her a feel—sunshot unbearable beach stink of mounded fish discarded for whatever reason only vultures know at Mocambo. Mocambo, white mosque hotel and arced swimming pool of underwater give her a crazy blow job. Oh Veracruz, sink back down into the sea and give me peace under the flickering lights, let me quietly and gradually take back with me everything that I came with—oh no, don't kill it—sink quietly, sun, and begin the promenade at Villa Del Mar and pineapples sprinkled with water from drip drop oh so clean black fingers—stop, I want to go back.

Back to the empty house. Hiss, the lizard smell of desertion. Everything stays as we left it. Every house we have ever stayed in, left, has retained its desertion for long periods of time. Washington, parkside up in the air, smell of magnolia trees the first day of spring and two white flowers now fertilize the ground of a parking lot that might have been there all along, level. So, Veracruz, N and B have taken ship and left Mexico for England—a peculiar new way to spend their pension—and left us all that good stuff, record player, typewriter, clothes, leather suede jackets, and a baby crib, not to speak of the manuscripts that always accumulate around whatever place we stay. Just as the going gets good, rather the staying, it is the end, and everything is abandoned. I want to go back to every place we have ever lived and retrieve all of everything left behind; surprisingly, it is most of it still there. It is all still there. Veracruz is still there, still suffering from the same lack of money, same depression and hard limes, same *parroquia* coffee and trolleys up and down the city round and crazy *arrista* bus goes *circumvalacion* just to spite its not-surprised passengers, buses take off in a whooping lark and twenty long in a row parade for me as I sit cool and fresh as possible in the newly found evening cool sipping something, looking. . . . Let me quietly and easily say my goodbye, deny despair, and leave Veracruz as untouched, as sweet as I found it. Goodbye, I want to die a little, in memory of you, Veracruz.

Goodbye to Ray arriving, carefree, in a taxi to intercept me before I find a trick to turn, because something better has come up. The D.A.—goodbye D.A., no more words spoken, I wish I had the power of payback to laud you with, but you are no doubt out of office, your white Castro shirts, though not discarded, decorate no more the jail of *frijoles segundas*. Ray was to get a private room in that jail with J's help so that we could fuck when I got back from Mexcity, but I didn't get back in time to see Veracruz defame Ray, call him a dope addict and communist and send him off to Mexcity, while I was still there, to pine in the same patio jail courtyard with two foot overhang, no more to shelter the whole jail population from the elements, including Fidel Castro who carves his initials in an educated hand, newly arrived from Veracruz, goodbye.

I have had good reason to regret the wild goodbye I took of Veracruz—cut off before I had even said hello hardly—when I opened the door to that dry dusty house and the señora from the store, knocked at the door, had come immediately when she saw me arrive. I thought she wanted the money we owed her so I start talking friendly, but I had already opened the letter. The vulture was already sitting on my shoulder and I almost fainted with despair, my blood stopped running at these words from Ray under the door.

Dear Bonnie— August 8

I am in Webb County jail, Laredo, Texas, under arrest for unlawful flight. I am very weary and bewildered. I hope this letter gets to you right away, and that you're still there to receive it. I expect to be here ten days or two weeks. . . .

Bond has been set at 10,000 dollars which, of course, I don't have. Please come if you are able and write to me—none of that "you-have-nothing-to-say" stuff; I need you just like I needed you yesterday and always . . . at any rate, don't despair over what is happening. . . . I am not, and I love you so much, as you love me. . . . What else is happening, I don't know; this has been all so fast. . . . Find a way to get here somehow as soon as you can and give me some courage! Write immediately. I have no money, no hope, and nobody... except you and Rachel... and I adore you both....

Sorry this is short... I will not be able to write again... have not even got seven cents for a stamp... how can I make 10,000 dollar bail-bond? Think of me; they let me keep your picture and I look at you....

Book Two

MEXICO TO LAREDO: GETTING RAY OUT OF JAIL

... From a letter written to me in Nuevo Laredo, Mexico sent by Ray from the Webb County Jail in Laredo, Texas.

> "... tell me some sexual items ... draw up a plan, a plot, a sequence! Start alone, self-sex, then me, then he, then he or she and so on! Your limits? Define yourself, time yourself, breaking point-weary? Write me information, so I know. ... Big 10, twelve hour scherzo, fill with progression—items, train, daisy-chain, swell to inconceivable cosmic finality ... Wagner, up-tempo, multiplication ... what you can stand and sit and walk and run and lie still for! Pow! Funk with a slunk! Probably several hundred coition points possible in a twelve hour symphony! Make your flesh delirious for me, but unperformed without me!"

So here I am again. I have gotten just a little bit higher, haven't I? You can't deny now when you say to me, "Don't you think it hurt things for you to run away to Mexico like that?" I am without an answer, my defenses down, but it is better like that, for something has awakened.

Mention drugs? Why yes, doctor, I managed to heighten the climaxes quite a bit with border-bought drugstore pills, but I have discovered, doctor, that analysis of drug effects goes up in a whirl even faster than specific problems attributed to general people, and when you start to speak of whether something should have been or shouldn't, try to consider my feelings for a change.

Distraction—I can't figure where to start—a chick on the make to get her husband out of jail—not just that—brought back to a country I had hoped never to see again. I am violently afraid of the United States and Texas, but I am coming to you fast, Ray, like a tornado, fast as every irregular bag of tricks I can muster will get me there. Gotta get there fast, Ray might not last. I fuck a border Mexican cop and make it across the border illegally on a bus full of Mexican shoppers—I don't care. That was the first time I ever fucked someone for something other than money or love. I had been informed at the ten-mile checkpoint that I could not cross the border, for my papers had expired and I didn't have the baby with me, and the immigration officials were waiting for me at the Nuevo Laredo bus stop. I had tried to con the bus driver to let me off early, but he wouldn't have anything to do with it though sympathetic and I was taken immediately to the chief of the immigration who tells me that I will have to go back to get the baby in Veracruz before I can even talk to him about crossing the border—meanwhile Ray is waiting desperate and I am wild to get to him, there must be some solution to this and I must somehow get to see him immediately, tonight. It is growing dark and I am in a complete panic, everything is so much already thoroughly out of whack; the end of the world has come. I tell him I have no money to return to Veracruz and I will have to wire my mother for it, so I am put in a hotel right next to the customs station. I wonder about chances of turning a trick in this forsaken atmosphere, am admitted to the hotel and I call my mother, who refuses to go to get the baby for me, but sees that she has to send me the fare to go myself. I drink a Coca-Cola, take a shower, send the hotel owner's son to pick up my letter from Ray in Laredo, which cools me a little, decide that I will go out to look around, nothing to lose. The sun has set, my dress is wool and I am immediately sweating. I have in mind to go again to see the chief of immigration and beg him to let me cross to see my husband in jail; he is not there, but the officer I talk to, in a very confidential sort of way, says that it can be fixed up. I lay it on the line, I am desperately in love and will do anything I can to see my husband, he asks me to walk across the street to the back of a parking lot where he will pick me up in his truck; we don't want to be seen. B the cop became our friend, for this was the biggest favor I ever fucked for. B took me to dinner somewhere out of the city where I was introduced to the local music and deliciousness of roast goat with good tortillas. He says to me that I will not be able to stay in my hotel room that night for "they will be looking for me." I am afraid he is going to pull an inhuman burn, but the risk must be taken at this point, so as he gets drunk, we dance, then drive through the flat and dry night, sounds of dogs and the city gaiety, always something happening there to amuse the passers-through, into the cricket cool of a deserted motel where two-story-high-up room awaits my baggage of green dress and suntan and somehow hardship-savored flesh grows not to mind his sympathies though he was one of the hardest lays to cope with I have ever come across, a definite streak of what I immediately term as fag, insisting on my meticulous administrations to his asshole. Although he is attentive and even reverent of my body, I somehow connect his demands with the most masculine of attitudes, even reminding me of Ray's, although that might have been due to the circumstances.

B falls asleep finally, satisfied and drunken. He has come on very affectionately through the whole thing, and I am inclined to accept it with as much good grace as I can muster, for I am putting all my money on getting across the border in the morning, but I am left the rest of the night with my doubts, so separate from everything, Ray across the border, Rachel in Veracruz, the shock only one day old, a letter in my bosom portends prisons and death. Morning dawns brilliantly hot with no sea breeze or hope of escape from the heat; it suits my mood, this hole is a perfect place for Hell. B wants me to have breakfast. I object, but he insists, and he is no person to argue with, so I do, the doubts growing in my head, but finally he tells me, "I am going to stop the jeep along this road here, this is where the bus to Laredo starts, all you have to do is get on and sit low down in the seat so you won't be recognized when it stops this side of the bridge—I am going to drive along behind so I will know if you make it or not, good luck." I thank him with all my heart, thank him, though I had done my part of the deal and the bus is off, my heart is in my throat, we are through the dusty streets of Nuevo Laredo. I feel the eyes of Mexicans on me, I am paranoid that everyone knows what is happening, through the checking points of customs, this is a regular shopping bus trip, Mexicans can go over for a day with no problem....

And they treated me so badly on the other side that I saw the "help" I had received from B in an even more romantic light and decided, when I got back to Veracruz that I would prefer to stay in Nuevo Laredo than ever put myself at the mercy of American ways of life again.

The street in the night in Laredo, after seeing Ray, after walking beneath his window in hopeful ritual circles, a prowl car circling me, it is white and scary, it thinks that I am going to stay around to jive with it, but I am on the alert, predict its movements and run when it is not in sight and make it into my hotel room just before it rounds the corner to see where I have gone. I cannot go back across the border yet, so I stay one night in Laredo, and watch the police search the empty lot beside my hotel with flashlights. Border town ballyhoo-sounds of the Rio Grande night, slap of water against the wetback thigh, two nations are at war, the border patrol has antennas and cruises the river marsh bank for the smell of marijuana plants grown from seeds lost from an immigrant pocket. The cop atmosphere here is unbearable. I see persecution as I never knew it existed. My citizenship is questioned every time I cross the bridge, though they are well-trained to recognize the difference between flavor and true nationality, they are better trained to offend and I put them on at every turning.

· · · · ·

Laredo is a vision of small-town horror with cheap department stores and several varieties of five and dime lining the streets. The streets are hot and bare and sterile, the Texans have no conception of being a part of the land: all spaces of earth or trees have signs saying keep off, and the remainder is a continuous vista of paved concrete, starting with the "international bridge" which has a dividing marker in the middle of the Rio Grande which is supposed to suggest some mutual amity, but it is all a farce signed by Roosevelt, the whole thing, the Mexican half included has been built and monsterized by capitalism, the dream ends on the south side where Mexican immigration facilities have not kept up with the times of the new bridge and still look like a sleepy bus depot as opposed to the forsaken Laredo customs which resembles F.B.I. headquarters. . . . I file through from the shopping bus crowd and look an American policewoman with florid mouth in the eye, saying I have just been across for a couple of hours. I breeze through, while an honest Mexican behind me is questioned vulgarly about his life.

The post office building and courthouse areas are meccas of American stature—the post office is the more impressive of the two for it is the FEDERAL ideal, housing the Federal Courthouse as well, as opposed to Webb County Spittoon Jail and Courthouse properties of trees. The Federal agent who arrested Ray (get out of Mexican deportation truck on the other side of the bridge still in Mexico: "What's happening?" "Just walk, across the bridge." Ray walks across the bridge, internationally free, all the concrete of the bridge between him, the world, and the sky, concrete creaks in border nightmares of plank bridge lost and floated away floodwise down the river. So Ray walks across the bridge a free man, and on the other side a Federal agent, a youth, taps him on the shoulder saying, "Ray Bremser?" and flips his credentials eye-high from out of his certified rump equipage. Ray jumps with surprise, "Oh Lord, don't shoot!" Oh wail, baby, put alla them gringos on)—this same agent receives me in his brick office of no interest, brick-front, professional, one-purpose building, flat on the street and midway sterile between Webb County plaza of processless law and the Federal beehive building of enormous post office flag so high you can see it from the other side of the river. His building is graceless of trees, the front door is inscrutable glass like the shithouse window on a train—I find Ray's case documented with no more than a paper signed by himself, not even original, which makes no official charge, no warrant from New Jersey or Webb County, just a little memo, which, signed by his federal hand, has already doomed us. He tells me pleasantly that he recommended $10,000 bail, I point out that he is completely out of order and am appraised by his federal eye.

· · · · ·

The señora from La Telepa had insisted that I go to the American Consul even before I found out how the baby was—kids ran down to fetch her from her house—the whole neighborhood down to the last scroungy dog is involved in the fall of our household. J appears, but I leave her on the step unheeded because I am going to see the American Consul immediately. I didn't want to see him, but then thought maybe he would have something pertinent to say, so the señora, my creditor and most jealous admirer of baby Rach (who tried to tell me in the taxicab bad things about J, and how the baby should not be with her), got a taxi and drove me to the American Consulate, by the water, on the Malecón, near the lighthouse and fancy apartments of the fresher and more presentable part of the city. The señora intends to go in with me but I send her home and ring on the "at home" section of the Consulate doorbells; a woman answers and speaks English. I am left standing on the doorstep while she goes to get her husband; having received my name, the Consul comes five minutes later, still getting himself together. His name is Black or Jeeves or something equivalently stupid, I note at the time. He greets me at the door, "oh yes, Mrs. Bremser," leads me through the darkened secretarial room of the building, not bothering to turn on the lights (saving electricity?) as he goes ahead of me. "Come in here, Mrs. Bremser"—the light is on in a very small room with a large desk and one straight chair opposite where I sit. I say I want to know about my husband immediately as I am in something of a rush. He has opened the conversation with questions about the robbery Ray is known to have committed and why he did it. I figure since he has nothing better to win me over with that the conversation was going to be a flop. I am looking for information. He starts to give me sympathy and I reject it saying my husband hasn't done anything and intimate that he is a better man than the Consul by far. Playing the game to the hilt, I ask him how I am going to get to Texas to find my husband. He says I will be sent by the American Consul by bus to Laredo. And suppose I don't want to go that way? "The Veracruz police are looking for you, Mrs. Bremser; you would be doing a very foolish thing if you try to get to Laredo by yourself, you will be arrested by the Veracruz police as soon as you go out this door and I won't lift a finger to help you then. We've been watching you for a long time. You and your husband (the way you dress!) have stuck out like sore thumbs; this is a small town." I interject my own private opinion of his public stature; rising from the chair, he says, "you'll be arrested." I find my own way out through the dark rooms with him pursuing and keeping up with the talk I no longer listen to. I pause at the door and tell him loudly that his wife is a whore and spit on his doorstep in passing and walk out into the Veracruz air, night thunderstorm breaking. I am free, my thoughts are my own, in the night air I am alone and the rain soaks me as I walk to the telegraph office, crying, thinking, unheeding, planning for our escape out of this. Fuck the American Consul, I telegraph Ray I am on my way babe, hang on.

When I get back to the Avenida Jiménez, J, who has had charge of the baby since Ray was taken to Laredo, clues me that I shouldn't have had anything to do with the señora from the grocery store La Telapa because it is she who has instigated the police against us anyway.

As I enter her house my first impression is of Rachel's face. I am immediately full of joy at seeing her and I do not take much notice of other circumstances for a ten minute blank of mind of complete enjoyment of her company. She doesn't know what is happening, she has been well cared for, but has a slightly pained blank look on her face of death, something like when she returned from Acapulco and it is all my joy to obliterate it. I cry with joy—being close to the baby in my arms is as close to Ray as I can get at the moment.

I try to tell J about the American Consul, but she knows already, she knows that the first thing I should do is get what I want to save from out of our house before someone goes there looking for me. So we are off on our first escapade, up to the house and by candlelight tear down the precious photographs, grab the manuscripts, typewriter, fill one trunk full and get what J will need to take care of the baby, or me. That and all other questions have not been answered yet. Let this herald the coming of the witch.

Veracruz night of sifting black dust; the rats belie the house and spiders do not scurry; even the dark ghost barely makes his presence known. No, more quiet so that the señora does not come from next door, I can hardly report to her my conversation, nor do I doubt that she already knows it from the American Consul himself, as she has a telephone. So quietly gather together what Rachel and I want to take with us into our next lives. I wonder, will I ever come back and pay the rent, but I am already too aware of the nature of arrests to believe it. So see the worst and do the most direct and forward things so as to catch up with it and have a word. I am in a hurry to be in Texas from the moment I open the door that afternoon. How we are made to sacrifice against our will, willingly we continue, so hurry and speak with him of our death, true communion.

Dark night shroud us as we tiptoe back to J's in the grass patch street of black dust. Lurking boys sent from the señora to spy on us leaving rustle in dark doorways beneath the trees and never appear to our expectations.

We arrive back at bright light house where the baby is still oodleycoo on grandma's knee rocking, being her sweet self comforted. J shuts up all the shutters so their neighbors can't see us, but the witch, where is she? J speaks to me, we do not understand each other, but we both know the issues at hand. We decide that it would be better for me to leave the baby behind for they will be looking for a woman with a baby.

The witch mesmerized up out of a fog in my head and as we open the shutter doors a heavy cloud of what I have learned to know as copal was rising furiously out of a small burning brazier on the floor. Somehow the baby's face floating on the incense, a bony old hag on the other side of the burning smoke gesticulates motionless the stopped moment that we came in the door, catching her in the act. I am somehow not supposed to have seen this, J and the old grandmother appear to me by their expressions to have been more participants than spectators who are the very young and the old. I am distressed enough to feel a need for someone's powers beyond the natural, in fact J had asked me (telling me that she knows a woman who can see into the future). She has a solution to my ills and offers it to me, did I want her to call in this old woman who was very wise, and

I said yes, but this suspended dance of abandon awakens a natural prejudice in me, so close to the baby, but the American Consul and police and New Jersey are a host of archfiends I think I can use some help with, so J and I ask the old woman questions. The commentary she gave on our future was this: I would never see Ray again—that I was going to be arrested on my way to Texas—that if I left the baby behind I would never see her again. In fact this was just a rundown on the total tragedy she foretold for us, so in spite of seeing the worst, she awakened completely fears in me that had only been threatened already—oh, this night in Veracruz took everything out of me, and yet I have to go on, going in the one direction you know you must and doing the best you can. I have no plan, but I know where I'm going; I am free of choices, being wanted by the police also.

In a cab, J and I are off to the bus station to get me a ticket for the next bus to Mexcity. I wait in the taxi while she goes to buy it for me, and comes back saying that the ticket seller when he heard my name, even from J, who undoubtedly showed him her credentials or more likely had even known him all her life, told her that he would not sell a ticket, that the public conveyance of bus and train had been notified that I was wanted by the police and was not to be allowed to leave the city. J tells me to keep my head down in the back seat, she asks me if I have enough money to take the cab to Mexcity and takes me looking for someone to drive. We shuttle in and out through the city stopping in many of my old haunts, me with my head down in the back of the car, J taking care of business. She cruises all of the *sitios de taxicab* in Veracruz, discreetly posing the problem to those she knows to be cool and either turning down or getting turned down on the proposition. Finally she finds one and we transfer to his car and go to pick up his wife. I am ready to go, my bag is packed, I am only carrying a straw thing with some poems in it. I remember now, it is all unnatural, the expression on my face is always of pain or anxiety, caused by the turmoil in my head. It is insane to be so alone and recognize it suddenly.

How can I recognize or remember the blue haze of night under the quiet trees when I was so unnaturally dealt with? How to be close to nature, or be a post and grow closer to nature so as to fight back? Twist your head so that what is far away is close and whether other people accept the truth of it or not it is your base to fight from and they will no doubt believe when you have done—the life will show, just as the dance writes a figure which is readable and has meaning.

Swiftly dancing to Xalapa—J and the rest of the taxicab entourage, I had agreed to pay the driver 500 pesos, everything I had in my pockets except what I had sent to Ray in the mail, not yet delivered, this and all other mail money I consign to J for the care of the baby. The taxicab driver is going like a crazy man on the roads, am I not in a hurry? And I have paid for speed, so speed, my friends kill off the beer and I sit back in the seat and let the wind blow in my face, so much to think about that I do not think, I am pure emotion. J puts her fat arm around me. He didn't do anything, it's all a lie, *mentirosos* all of them. She knows and confronts me as I cry. J found the pot that Ray had left on the table and had taken it home with her, somehow seeing the full implications of everything and doing everything she could to help. She gave Ray money in the Veracruz jail and had arranged for a private room for him to await me in—conjugal visits where the wife can live in the local jail and go in and out as she pleases, the prisoners sit around in a courtyard smoking pot and eating the most delicious *gordas* Veracruz has to offer, but he was sent away immediately to spend a short time in the Mexcity jailhouse. I don't say exactly that I think every case in law where someone is sent to jail is an example of injustice, as I know ours to be, but I am sure it is 90% true, and the state things are in since I have been alive is that all offenses punished by the state are brought on by the state in the first place, but only after jail does the canker become evident. Someone can commit rape or murder or most of the other crimes *purely* and come to whatever reconciliation with nature is necessary. That is justice. I refuse to be guilty; let us suffer the penalties from beginning to end and it will only be a more beautiful mark on our lives.

Xalapa, in the state of Veracruz, or Jalapa, once you get into the hills is a condition of cultivated jungle, the road winds like the outside border of a garden in and out of hollows whose purpose is to contain banana trees and coffee bushes growing evergreen around the trunks. The houses all have flowers, the huts and shacks of poverty are beautiful, the flowers fitting gracefully into the roadside. But it is night, and my joy is speeding over the roads and curves, we seem to almost crash a couple of times, but it is apparently more of the Veracruzano taxicab driver's bravado, so that I find it kind of a sympathy directed towards me. I feel that this driver is really trying to get me there fast because I want to see my husband. The purpose of going to Xalapa is to see the man that I had visited in Xalapa with J before, in fact this is the third time I have come directly to him. J had brought me there unannounced two weeks earlier and asked him to give me money so that I could have a birthday party for the Rach. He had been more than courteous in his office at that time, talking to me as a friend the same as he did J, and giving me 200 pesos, which had paid my busfare and circumstantial money needs for the trip to Mexcity; how I wish now I hadn't gone, maybe together we could have gotten rid of the Mexican police, maybe I could have done one of them, or killed both of them and fled to Guatemala, more trouble perhaps but maybe we would have succeeded in protecting our lives, I had always vowed after we ran away from Hoboken that should anyone try to arrest Ray again they would have a violent scene on their hands. And now I had missed that opportunity, and, in fact, they used my absence to lure Ray into their hands, telling him that I had been in a bus crash and that they wanted to take him to me at the hospital, so he came out of the house and they grabbed him and took him to the Veracruz jail. The legality by which he was held was that his tourist visa was expired. The means the F.B.I. had used to interest them in Ray was telling them that he was a drug addict and a communist, those two offenses the most comprehensible to nervous Mexican officials, and most often used whether any offense exists or not. But my papers are out of order, too, so J is going to plead for me with this man to write me a letter to the government in Mexcity, which he had offered to do before, so that my visa might be extended in time without my having to go to the border to do it, and now we approach him in this emergency to try to keep me out of jail.

The taxicab arrives at his gateway—a wall around his house contains a doorbell, J rings, and calls, "*licenceado*," the title she gives him, her call is answered finally and we are left waiting for him to put a shirt on, J points through the bars and indicates a jasmine bush to me, I am so close to the point of constant tears, this gesture of hers makes a permanent impression of sweetness on me, but I doubted then that I would ever live to enjoy it in memory. I don't want to enjoy it in memory, I want to go back and watch that actual bush grow.

The *licenceado* appears fully clothed, his shoes shiny. I somehow admire him, and this meeting adds to the pleasure of our friendship, it is three in the morning and he has gotten out of his bed, glad to see us, ready to listen to J, who is excited about something he can see, and listens to the story she tells, and asks me a couple of questions I answer in halting Spanish, and goes into the house again to write a letter for me, which didn't ever do much good but only because his connections in Mexcity were not as courteous as he. He wishes me luck, and I wish that I might overcome all of this to see him again some day, but the thought is a remote one, the possibility a distant one, and so I say goodbye to another friend.

So I take my leave of J, she will return by bus, I give her back her rubber plastic sandals which decorate my feet like a garden trellis, J with a border of fat brown and beautiful flesh, nothing has aroused in my mind more friendship than that color of brown—she is with the suggestion of a well-cultured soul to match it. I left with her half my household, the baby, I trusted her that well. I cry goodbye to Veracruzana Mamma J, go well, *que tu via bien*, and I am off with no money in my pocket, no assurance but my need to get to Laredo, no company but the husband and wife in the front seat who leave me to my despair in the back and only drive diligently through and across and around, the dark night way, *mysterioso* valleys and guided by stars I have not paid any attention to yet, which anyway watch down on me as I sleep.

Oh, I am sick with anticipation as we arrive in Mexcity, early morning at the edge of the city, though this means I am probably free of the police, I have no money to even get someplace within the city, the entrance into Mexico City from *circumvalacion* areas of buses pouring in and trains circling and stopping, is a far walk from the areas of town that I know even slightly, and I have no money, not even to take a bus, and I am cold to the bone.

One stop in the night my drivers had awakened me to ask if I wanted coffee so we went into a little night-side cafe with decorations of many religious pictures, and a little girl of ten serves them coffee and a meal while I sit at a separate table, digging her character from her face, one thing I notice in all of this tension of having to deal with problems too complex to work at more than slowly and hope to endure the pressure meanwhile, is that if you care to look, if you try to get out of yourself for just a moment and open your eyes to other people, someone's guard is down and things appear more clearly. The little girl looks at me wonderingly. When we leave the proprietor wonders whether to charge me standard prices for the coffee, but is paid for by the cab driver, some kind of health is drunk all around, beyond my comprehension.

I am finally told, needlessly, that we are approaching Apizaco, that we will be in Mexico City in an hour. I see by the mud huts that this is a kind of civilization growing up to our approach, the sun is up. South of us back down and beyond Tehuacán, Indian mushroom people live each day as if their lives were gifts which they in turn dedicate to the mountain and the mushroom. Directly behind Veracruz rises a mirage above the insurmountable Popocatépetl and so I am truly closed in, there is no doubt it is morning and I have helped to drag it up in my head.

Once in Mexico City, rather at the edge of it, my driver is now turning back to Veracruz, and having taken 50 dollars he gives me back

MEXICAN MEMOIRS

50 cents so that I can continue my journey into town, I am going to Roger B's house where I think I will be safe from the police until I get my papers straightened out—Plaza Citlaltépetl, homeless and passionless I get no expired papers. I am out in the hot Mexcity muggy afternoon, more determined than before to have things my own way, and nothing inspires me better than resistance at this point. I am still reading Castro and know that all petty shifts and loopholes that end up in favor of the government are always illegal. So, down the street, swinging it only mildly in rebellion, my head goes up even higher. I call Emanuel de la G in a little restaurant where I am taunted for some unknown reason by the proprietor, oh bug me good everybody, for I will make it through this so much much better being bugged, it is natural that I should be bugged, the more so the better, get my energy up in a passion. It is easy to explain things to Emanuel de la G, for he has known the situation, and I must only add the small facts of the tragedy and impress him with the expensiveness of my escape from Veracruz, that I must continue my trip to Laredo, and he tells me to come by his office and promptly presents me with 200 pesos and wishes me good luck.

I am in a perpetual state of sweat, the elements have met my arrival in Mexcity with a burst of heat, I do not look or wish for pleasant weather, have no prospects of pleasure and so continue this soul drive in the withering heat, but do not wither.

Back to Roger's I mail, or package to mail, and extract a promise from M that she will promptly mail Ray's manuscripts to him in Laredo, remember I am forecast an answer to my knock in the morning, frantically I try to think my way out of it. This is the situation: Ray is in Laredo, I hope, (I have had but one letter dated five days earlier), the baby and home are behind me, I have no money to go backwards or forwards or even to move around in the city, no money, so I am left the alternative of asking for help. I call M, a friend who helped us escape to Mexico in the first place. In a short time she introduces me to a friend, R, whom I coerce with my story for money. I don't consider this a fault. M is shocked that I make such an open thing of the circumstances and probably thinks that I am playing on people for their pity, but the truth is when this person asked me a couple of questions touching on two subjects, my husband and my baby, I just spilled the whole thing, so distressed that to talk about it is only the natural wringing out of anxiety, and this person, R, shaken by the immensity of horrible detail, could not but help. My mistake was later to get high at Roger B's house (mistake to be myself? What am I, a statue?) and spill the beans about how we have supported ourselves these months in Veracruz. Maybe I bait M a little for she has been shocked already at R's house, and I am surprised at her disapproval and so continue to lay more of the whole story on her than I should have, bitterly boasting, not at all reconciled at things, wondering at the necessity of the past myself, this present necessity being so much greater. Anyway, I pour out a confession that burns their ears and covers up my human tracks. I have begun to erect a reputation that will make my personality and my love a recluse, though both are there to be seen.

That was a busy day, the one of my arrival into Mexcity. R's father was a lawyer, and she recommended him to me, and me to him, for I had a plan I wanted to verify with someone. I was very worried about the baby with J, that she might not fare well, as I had to keep free—and that J would in spite of her credentials of authority not be able to cope with the American Consul—so I went to see Mr. B in his office and told him that I wanted to swear out a paper giving Rachel to J until I was able to return to Veracruz to get her. He told me that such a paper would be useless, that the sensible thing for me to do would be to return to Veracruz immediately and get her, but he made the paper for me anyway and witnessed it, and I had it photocopied and sent a copy to J. I think that all of this maneuver was incomprehensible to anyone but me, and didn't work technically, but it left me free enough in my own mind. I must do all the way what I think is best, for how can I continue to face these obstacles? I remember feeling as if I were contracting some great treaty.

I was finally admitted to Roger B's house and invited to stay, in fact M was staying there then. Roger's house was full of people and bedbugs. I poured out to them my whole story and they reacted variously. Roger was very sympathetic. Blonde Spanish Roger, Ray and I had stayed with him on a previous trip to Mexcity, a lark, an explorative journey to Mexcity to initiate me to hustling there, but I was sick the whole time and had to go to a local clinic to be treated for kidney infection, on a street where other doctors' offices were located, one where I had my abortion, not wanting to have a baby so obviously belonging to the streets, our matrimonial vows already so abused. I am hardly yet able to face this specter of murder, and how much better would things have been then if I could have accepted the fruits of my labor, good and bad, since I am not much of a judge of which is which now. But Roger was nice enough to be able to understand my frantic state, and that night I was introduced to the first taste of something called Acapulco Gold, which was not the real thing; I did not run into the authentic item until three years later in New York, and it is something like wheat grain, beautiful healthy high, but these kids at Roger's were smoking something good, and I helped them, and sat up through the night writing a huge slow letter to Ray including as much encouragement and love to him as I could.

Most American tourists have to pay a 500 peso forfeit for arrest at the border, for myself I take all possible precautions.

I see O that night and receive his revolutionary encouragement, I have called him to ask if there is any way I can cross the border and avoid the officials, he tells me of the illegal crossings he made during the revolution, and I decide that it will not be hard. I look at the map when he tells me that in Reynosa you can walk across the riverbed and avoid customs altogether, but it is too far a detour, he tells me that customs are less stiff by train than by bus, but I decide to take the bus anyway. The afternoon has been lost for me . . . I call New York City, a shot in the dark, our patron there knows people in Texas and will try to get a lawyer for Ray. She is appalled at the injustices, too, so confident and scared, I board the bus to Laredo and the adventure is begun.

Mexcity, D.F., hot morning and I have slept a couple of hours of exhausted sleep. M and her visiting girlfriend are making American scenes together, maybe going house-hunting, there is a kind of middle class drive evident in them that they do these chores during the day that I have never been able to experience in my whole life, devoted to more ethereal cares or joys. The girl is in love with an Argentinean boy who is younger than she and who has proposed, and the whole business with M's encouragement becomes one of a cliquish type of sorority friendship. They are all sympathetic towards me, and I am introduced to a wardrobe of clothing that one of the revolutionary chicks who had stopped at our house in Veracruz with Marc S has left behind, so I borrow the best of it to put to my specialized uses and carefully dress to go to *gobernación* where I arrive amidst federal trees and employees dressed identically, set up for a killing identically. I am later to see these types as a particular whorehouse grouping, the way they lounge on the *gobernación* lawns and stoned patios. The person to whom I have been directed by J's friend is named Dr. L and after I am kept waiting for an hour he arrives and gives me an interview, reading the letter my friend has written, and he makes no favorable response except to express his sympathy. He is a little fat man, I have some idea that if I turn on the charm it is going to make a difference to this man in this ground story patio, seemingly private office, but I wonder why if he is so influential, he is in this ground floor, crowded office. But when he tells me that it will not be possible for me to get a new visa issued, I doubt him, start to fill him with pitiful details, and beg and plead (although I did not mention the part Ray is playing in things, somehow thinking this was cool). My papers being in the shape they are, I am sent to the Secretary of *gobernación* to straighten it out. I somehow hope that I am getting special attention, not because the case has already come to their attention, but through my letter of introduction. The morning is dragging out, I am standing on sidewalks here and there, looking American already with the new store-bought clothes.

The secretary is entertaining visitors. His office is gorgeous, balcony high, cool in the morning heat; the place is gloriously dark, impractical for paperwork but suitable for his position, and his faggot combination secretary door-boy and water-boy is dignified. I have been ushered up by Dr. L, on the agreement that if the secretary is willing he will go against the rules in my case, this is the amount of his courtesy to my friend's intro: to make another introduction. I think that now I am really getting somewhere, we wait ten minutes outside the door but are admitted in the midst of the other interview which consists of foreign dignitaries and newspaper men. Dr. L knows everyone by the first name, I try to size up the scene and come on where it will help, and am introduced to one of the famous reporters and put in a hardship smile, and answers to questions of my problems I have not ventured to the officials yet, but I am barking up the wrong tree. I am introduced to the secretary of *gobernación*, in Dr. L's presence, who shortly leaves for he is so busy, the secretary starts to beat around the bush and I proceed to lay it on the line, thinking that further involvement of my story with trouble will soften him, but the outcome is shortly evident. I am to have ten days to leave Mexico, not at all what I had hoped for, though this makes my presence legal it does not in any way help me, but only puts new pressure on my getting out. I do not want to be expelled, I want to rescue Ray and have hope of getting back immediately, but the rubber stamp is out before I can object and the friendly help I was to have received has been a waste of time, and I suspect that the situation is now even worse.

Though before it was a place, Veracruz, the beaches, post office, house on Revillagigedo, morning breakfast at the plaza, now it is more centralized: the jailhouse, in Laredo morning. I am chafed by duties keeping me away, I want to walk there every moment of the day, check and make sure that Ray is O.K.

And it is up again at every turn, I vow I will live, and what's more, I vow that I will live to tell it. Limited literary means nothing, there is something important to say and it will out and I won't miss any opportunity to call back the pain and put the blame where it should lie. I am not going to go through life and let stuff sit on my back passively, especially when it still bugs me, yes, at every opportunity it comes back to bug us.

So the baby must immediately be rescued. Passing back the way I came, the head of immigration on the opposite side, Nuevo Laredo, chides me for escaping from but it has already been done, and he is in the position of having to give me in retrospect what I have already taken, so I return with a new visa to Veracruz, quickly, forcing connections, by bus. I see faces already I have come to know, and notice their looks of encouragement, and admiration; this is the Mexican principle of self-protection, and their acceptance means somehow that we will come back the victors. I take in Mexico's surface like a face going back to Veracruz. I do not notice the towns, I notice the spaces and gauge the speed of our passage over them by picking up landmarks, watching the approach of a plateau or valley, sitting forward in the bus seat to encourage the bus to faster flight, sixteen hours to Mexcity and I am immediately on another bus to Veracruz, eight hours later I am there, my excitement preceding to the house of J. I grab the baby Rachel and her accessories, give hurried words of goodbye, and they are heartbroken to lose the baby. E wants to come back with me, but I don't have the money for her fare. I promise to write and send her fare to come join us, and we are immediately back into the bus and back again to Mexcity.

So back into Nuevo Laredo and various musics intermingle across the river. The sun is unbearable. It is different to walk through the streets with the baby Rachel on my arm, I am already feeling acquainted with this town, the head of the immigration greets me, takes me into his office as usual for a little talk. I always have the feeling that he is on the verge of making a proposition, he has several times come close to accusing me of whoredom, but I comment on the pictures of children on his desk, under glass, tell him that I plan to live in Nuevo Laredo for a week or so and travel into Laredo. I rush immediately to the jail, to find that visits are limited to twice a week, two days out of the week any time during the day. With the baby I go to see Ray at the concrete window. It is a hot void, and I hardly recognize him. What are we doing here? My mind is in total confusion.

Disjointed dreams when I do sleep, but most of the time I am frantically up every night writing letters to him, trying that way at least to keep things together. For reasons unknown, they won't accept my letters to Ray half the time. They pass them from hand to hand among pinochle-playing guards, who are Mexicans who have sold out to the States somewhere along the way and retain none of their heritage. The rules are to be imposed from one direction only, from the law down, and they use that as a front behind which to play pinochle and eat up the food that is supposed to be given to the prisoners, as a result Ray is telling me, when he talks of the food, of amazing things like ten beans on a plate and one slice of bread with a taste of avocado spread on it. I am forced to buy food for him from my own lack of money regularly, every day, not because he wants luxuries but because, plainly, he is just not given anything to eat. I am constantly frantic with worry for the both of us, and try to get money from my mother, or Elaine de R, anyone I can remember the address of. I know that I will have to hustle, but the scene is very bleak and it will be a hard pull, especially with nobody to look after the baby. The streets are unreasonably hot with the Texas summer sun, and the baby and I suffer greatly walking miles to the jail, and we do that as often as we are able for it is the only sanity left in this place. We also walk to the lawyer's house, appointed by Roy F. He agrees to work for no fee, and I go there countless times, to protest, to beg, or to talk my franticness out.

I want to keep on fighting to the death, but calmly, Bonnie, light up a home roll and tell about a frantic trip out into the hot sun—even live it if necessary, but with open eyes, for it is all to go down here.

Rachel and I checked into a concrete structure called a hotel, far back from the border in Nuevo Laredo. I should always differentiate Nuevo Laredo from Laredo; I insisted on living on the Mexican side. I was afraid of the Texas police, and I wanted a better position from which to operate. After all, I have found it not too greatly illegal to hustle in Mexico, and even the head of immigration (though he has threatened that if I am caught causing any trouble in Nuevo Laredo that he would have to make me leave) has looked at me sympathetically. I know that the police on the American side would like to get me on anything. In fact, they are constantly threatening to put me in jail for just standing beneath Ray's window and talking to him, and they tell Ray that they are going to put me in jail and Rachel in an orphanage if I don't stop that, but I am stubborn, wildly defiant of any discipline so I do it even more often to bug them, I guess, and also just to be alone close to Ray. It was a long walk from our new concrete stucco hotel, and the windows out on some secondary plaza of Nuevo Laredo let in too much morning sun. Rachel lays in a basket, our baggage consists mostly of baskets. On the way back, final trip from Mexcity, the bus stopped in a dawn plaza of Indian basketry and I bought a covered basket to serve as a suitcase.

Once or twice I exceeded the friendship of B the cop, who considered himself my steady. Though he only gave me dribbles of money and help, I considered him my mainstay, mostly because of the insecurity of the police situation there, and I knew he was sympathetic. Nonetheless one late afternoon when I needed money badly, had nothing, funny to get down to not even Coca-Cola bottles to cash in a strange place. I get dressed in the freshest I got (and funny also how it is not up to me, but an attraction which occurs like Ray says, Monk eyeing the keys while someone else, probably Milt Jackson or John Lewis, is also up to something, and then it happens, like flies making it in midair), and a young man digs me on the street. I somehow find change to have lemonade in a patio parlor alone, so he can dig me better and approach. I am not often so cool, he is shy to the point of sweetness, and I think at first that he is too young, but a good possibility in this town of no visual hustle, everyone on the streets is busy hustling the Americans and I am not interested or able to try them yet (my prejudices). The young man asks to sit down and I allow him to join me. His youth is a motivation for me to set the price as soon as I can. I am nervous, he tells me how impressed he was by my entire profile in silhouette, like a queen, a young queen I think he specified, and I quickly find out his business, salesman, and his inclinations to pay me. He is short of money and reluctant at first to pay the 300 pesos I ask for, but when we get to his room, and we retire there immediately in the setting evening, I lay the whole story on him of the baby sleeping back in the hotel and Ray across the river, and he came across with what I needed. His room was in a triangular, jutting-out building, which I will come to know again later, slatted doors, sign of the tropics, tile hallways, double-centered windows. In fact his room is so full of windows we had to shut out evening with blinds to avoid the eyes of the adjoining market. I let myself go a little, he wants love (doesn't every one?), but he is young and better able to talk me into it. We somehow achieve a good enough fuck and unity through conversation that when it is done it is a clearing away of the day's cares, good healthy boy and girl fuck. He wants me to sleep there and give him more, but in my impatience to get away, my suntan naked persuasion, my means are twisted and he is more desirous of another good clean fuck. The second was an aftermath and reluctant for me, for I never want to do twice what I am getting paid for once, with no money in hand, though I have insisted that it be in sight on the table, because from there on I am capable of self-protection, so it was just a cool evening laying aside one another, no interesting perversions, just kiss and give a feel. Let him admire me, he gets hot again, there are some struggles of tension, and then it is in, up and down and over and I quickly dress and make arrangements to see him again sometime, and out, money in pocket. I have succeeded in taking care of business.

Oh, it is good to eat after several days of nothing but worry, and good to know that in the morning I will go to the jail across the bridge, no problem with the nickel toll; I will probably even ignore the tollkeeper as I pass and hitch the baby higher on my hip, and buy peaches for Ray, enormous ones that make a whole meal for our shrunken stomachs, and sit square down on the sidewalk between the courthouse and Ray's jail window, almost hidden by trees as it is by bars mesh of superfluous shading, sit there and eat the peach I have saved from Ray's and know that he is watching and know that his watching makes me hotter than any Laredo sun, the baby cooing among the grass roots of courthouse sprinkler lawn. Don't no one care, not till the sheriff comes along and I hear about it on our next visit. That's how it will be tomorrow, window Ray, the shadow god that leaves little more than a footprint on mirrors.

But now it is night and the creepy blueness comes to haunt me, the dull starless night. I know that Ray will be glad that I pulled this trick O.K., no burn, no fear, but the light of indescribable conscience shines at me from beyond the darkness I know lies over the river—maybe it was better to have no money and not wonder about this specter that I fear will be our downfall. Sure I have to take care of the baby, and I am proud that I can do it independently of American law, but the light and the dark still haunts me, I am so close to the brink of being ashamed, maybe because I liked it—this is an esoteric problem especially to bug me while Ray is in jail. The emptiness makes more sense to me than all of this nighttime flourish of tourist shop jade earrings and gaucho pants and beautiful puckered shirts, the emptiness below which stands for the roast goat I see in all the restaurant advertisements, the lost dog howl I never hear in town, no mongrel dog Mexico this, this is tourist-ville, and loneliness knowing even the Mexicans here are almost Americans. I eat, check Rachel, play music on the jukebox, and watch the other late-nighters.

The music is really too much for me to ignore; gaucho's gaiety accelerated to an amazing polka tempo getting faster and even more aboriginal in Texas even, poor Texas, as if it were occupied, cannot always maintain its square crew-cut, is swung out beyond its intention, way far out of its intention swings, but it is an underground sense that I have become used to picking up like the Indian continuation of life and music in Mexico—there is a doughnut place in Laredo, across from the post office but hidden by trees and a street that from the middle of the square (Laredo despite its intentions has a plaza also, which it mars by putting KEEP OFF signs up) dwindles off into intentional nothing, where truck drivers and Texan rummies scoff doughnuts and hear wild polkas sung by cowboys who have never seen a singing movie. So I linger there mornings on my dwindling American dimes, speak Spanish at every opportunity, implying the truth I am too paranoid to proclaim, knowing the weird fallout of Texas. Texas is the most vicious atmosphere I have ever suffered. We are into September already, two weeks in this place have lacerated and nearly killed us, we wait news about bail, wait news about a bail bondsman, and meanwhile try to do feeble damage to the enormous government of clerks and memos from Washington by pressuring the sheriff and his deputies who feature themselves total Texans and incorporate Mexican heritage they are anxious to deny and which I see as a mutual betrayal in them and love to bring to their attention. I call them wetbacks and turncoats, which they don't understand too well, and they reply, "we are more American than you are," and I silently say, "yeah man, and you can have it, too, you are fully welcome to your keep-off-the-grass parks and courthouse lawns which furnish me with the corrupted surface to spit on, having become the face of your earth, return me to the other side which, though also corrupted, is mine."

One afternoon, B the cop informs me that he has someone in town for me to meet and that he will pick me up that evening to take me there and that I should be nice to this guy as he is a friend of B's from businesses long back. It hits me that B is very experienced like Humberto O, the Mexican revolutionary, who has friends all over. So I fix myself up, anxious for something lucrative to come of this, and B and

I drive in his truck way out of town beyond bus routes, not talking much, knowing that this is not the night for our own personal pitch, neither of us coming on, except he with his friend, dual reasons for wanting me to make it here. He raises the pitch mightily as we get to the motel with the swimming pool, calls in by house phone, opens the door to the individual suite, which we are immediately introduced to as the bridal apartment, that phony. This cat was wearing a horrible ugly Hawaiian shirt which contrasts with his Batista Florida come-on of riches. He invites us in for drinks which B accepts, but I am so disgusted I poke B in the ribs, which he ignores. I am twisted into sitting on a bed and drink the Scotch he has given me, which I do not like either, and invited to converse; dinner is offered to both of us, but B professes business and intimates to leave me behind till he returns, I do not talk, only briefly and bugged answering questions directly put to me. We sit there for an hour or so, B leaning on a bed pillow keeps the conversation going in phony family business talk, they make some kind of deal business-wise friendly, making a big thing of trusting each other.

Through all this, which seems to have no real meaning, comes some kind of indefinite pitch from the disgusting dark cat who no doubt is driving a Cadillac (which later proved to be true. I sometimes sense a whole scene, my instincts are good); it turns out he is out of money and wants B to get him a check cashed, which makes the whole scene fall apart anyway, so that I am visibly justified in not wanting any more to do with even the person's proximity and start acting jively insistent with B to the point of insulting his friend and we all split together. He wants us to go in his Cadillac, which I nix, and we drive back to town with him following, B and I not talking at all, except that I am completely out of money, and smiling he lets me off at my hotel and gives me a couple of dollars loan, left alone with his own problem of the cat who is no doubt trustworthy, though it is funny in this instance he has to prove it.

...Another mysterious pickup late that night of need—back to the hotel with shuttered doors, a sneak entrance with me reserving the room and the cat who has something to fear from the public follows me in and fucks. I remember he was a creepy, short, fifty-year-old man, fag-looking type who fucked like a satyr—furious and wanted badly for me to suck him off, paid well for me to do it in the shower and likewise mysteriously disappeared from the room before my exit from it. I saw him later in town, he wanted me to be his mistress, which offer I absorbed with enthusiasm, for his wallet bulges were more healthy than I have ever seen on a walking person, especially a mark which he obviously was, and after he left I smoked a cigarette on the bed at his instructions not to leave immediately. The light is out, I am half-clothed, a timid knock at the door, it is the little brown, grown-up chiclet seller of the street I saw out front near the desk as I entered. I start to put him down to protect myself thinking he wants a free peek, but he offers me fifty pesos to do it—"do it"—I figure, oh well, to save trouble, and his brown cock in me, his head reaches the breast level of my prone front and he loves my nipples as if I were his mother. I keep my eyes peeled for attempts at him stealing my stash of pesos, but he is sincere, and pays....

Sometimes with all the excitement I lose track of what I am doing—like the second night in one of the hotels I stayed in. I asked the desk clerk to wake me the next morning and he asks me to leave the key in case I don't hear him knock, and I, in fact, never heard him knock but woke to sensations of a husbanded bed and though I wake slowly I see the boy there already undressed ready to jump in sitting on my bed playing. Arg, I up and scream at him and he is out the door half clothed before I am fully awake, my first fear for the baby. Alone in the world and disgusted, berated by Ray, for this, I have to move out super fast that day to protect my confidence. I had only moved in a day before after a bad scene at the last hotel where I awoke at dawn with a great hole burning by my head on the bed. So someone had given me a lead on a Casa De Huespedes, a boarding house where I got bed and two meals a day for fifty pesos a week, but it was well away from the border again. I had become used to roving in the center of town near the immigration gates, but I hire a horse drawn cart and get straight and move immediately.

So I have learned to lower my eyes and hide what I know—learned to pick up on what people thought I said instead of persisting in my own vulnerable blunder, have learned to turn on the vacuum so that people can express whatever outgoing tendencies they have toward me, and it is a strain, for I learned soon enough where it leads—to an endless involvement which I am forced to believe as valid as any other contact with people.

Letter to Ray:

> *. . . 11:30—Just got in, been walking for three hours, made the rounds looking for a familiar face to touch for money, but nothing, have to wait for Monday. I walked by the jail quietly because I felt you were uneasy, and up pops an old codger with a flashlight shining in my eyes. I shield them with my writing book and say, "what*

do you want?" He pipes in a crotchety voice, "I'm the guard of the courthouse and I have charge of all the grounds around it!!!" I say, "Well, what's the matter?" "What's your name?" he asks. I answer lowly, leaving him in silence (he doesn't want to betray his bad hearing, already lacking the virility of a fat rump, which is the badge and dignity of a real cop, and also the foundation of law enforcement, foundation on which rests the pistol proud and hard making up for what lacks in that other limp and useless tool) and he says, "Well, you come on with me. I want them to identify you around front, see if you're the same one they're looking for," so I say O.K. and he walks off while I light a cigarette. He gets ten feet away and discovers I'm gone and does a double take and then tries to take the double take back and squeaks gruffly, "Come on you and don't give me any trouble or I'm gonna arrest you," so I say, "O.K., O.K., don't get excited," and catch almost up to him and then slow down again. He's trying to hurry me, keeps turning anxiously to see if I'm still there and I say, "on what charges you gonna arrest me?"—he says "Well, we're going to walk around here and see if this guy recognizes you. You got any children?" I say, "What's that to you, old man?" and he is offended and, not knowing the dialectics of the beat 'em first, book 'em later philosophy, he says, "Well, of course you don't have to answer my question, but I just asked that one straight from me and it's a good honest . . ." I interrupt him: "But you're not in a good honest business, old man, and I don't plan to answer any questions." He does a double take again, not hearing right, and says indignantly, "Well, I don't know what questions you'd want to ask me. I'm a sheriff's deputy, I got my card right here, and you'd better be careful or I'm gonna arrest you right here and you won't even have a chance." So I am silent and we walk, slowly gaining the front corner of the jail yard and his sense of accomplishment grows as he starts to turn the corner. I stop and say, "I think you'd better go down to the police station and get a cop and arrest me then." He squeaks furiously, "But I am a cop! I been a sheriff's deputy for twenty-seven years." I say, "Well, let me see your papers then." He whips out a thin plastic ID case with one other card in it and I take it as he says, "See my pistol here?" He pats it and it flops like a toy, being very small, above his drooping buttocks. "I got a badge, too, look, with my name on it and everything." I bend close to look at it. It is one-half inch in diameter. I inspect his card; there is a space for a picture. I say there's no picture here, and look at it closer. He shouts, "But you don't have to have a picture! You better come with me to be identified or they're gonna pick you up tomorrow with a warrant!" I hand him his card and cross the street, saying, "Well, I'll wait till tomorrow then." "They're gonna git you," he says, and I walk back across the river. . . .

 I reach the second corner in North Laredo and take in an English conversation behind me, viewing the participants from the corner of my eye: a middle age, clean cut, suntanned Texas businessman, and a tall twenty-eight-year-old fellow who is probably his son, obviously a repressed homosexual, bulging waistline, amply rounded hips, crew-cut, who watches me walk while his father is talking and says, "Que bonito!" for my ears alone. I keep walking and the other guy keeps talking unheard and this cat (the one who is such great cop material) moves up behind and beside me thinking he's gonna score and speaking in English, thinking I have mistaken him for a Mexican, asking me something about the C.O.D. postal rate, thinking I *am a Mexican. I turn slightly toward him and spit juicily on his feet and he jumps back and angrily says, "I'd like to see you do that again—I'll kick you into the street!" and his father shuts up in confusion, sensing a dangerous international situation. All the Mexicans are watching, and I turn casually still walking and spit again and he calls me a goddamn whore and falls back, at which point I turn again and say loud and clear: "I'm not a whore! You're a pimp and a stupid American, and if you want to pick up a silly bitch on the street you'd better go back to the other side where you belong!"*

. . . And that was the last letter I wrote as our plans for suicide reached consummation. The next morning I go to the lawyer's side-street office; he has always permitted my most far out put-downs of personal property and even consented to most of them. He lives a leather-covered sofa life of shambled house and has a companion "friend," a young fellow with a Volkswagen and very motherly pipe-smoking face. But I don't care any more about them, my interest is exhausted, I have summoned myself to his burning afternoon-sun step with the baby too many times to be able to make it any more, and have been more impressed by the Mexican family across the street who rescued us into their house from one rainstorm. But I go, slowly, to see him, my routine, my walk of thoughts in the air, besides we already have a solution, we are going to die and my heart's eye is thusly fixed. Beyond other considerations, I do not even worry about the next meal anymore.

And he is waiting to tell me that the bondsman has arrived and is going to get Ray out today; I should go see him at such and such a place.

TROIA

Damp wind across the river and ominousness in the air. Baby Rachel is at M's. M runs a beauty parlor in the neighborhood near the red-light section of the town. It is too bad I do not remember the real Mexican border name for this three square blocks of Orphic song, but I connect it with the name Lolo which rings in my head like a guitar string. B the cop took me there one night looking for him so we could hear him sing, a street singer, Lolo, of this three block square area of bright lights, advertising a happy night of visiting in this or that house, no discretion necessary in this open scene of welcome if you are an American with money or a Mexican hustler of some sort, but don't be anything in between, except as I was, with an official escort. Anyway, M's beauty parlor used to house the baby and also I took my wardrobe there for it to be washed and ironed, all for very little money, though I never got complete devotion like in Veracruz. No, Nuevo Laredo was a mixed scene and, as sensed all along, a precarious one for me and Rachel, but at least more sure than that in Laredo. That would have been beyond comprehension, we would have had to beg at the doors of the Salvation Army or Catholic Charities, which I considered a couple of times anyway, and tried the blood bank which never works, should be the other way around, I should have gone for a transfusion.

I am wearing the blue French hustler's beret given to me by Marge C in Hoboken, one of those tokens of friendship in my life, like the amethyst ring I gave Malcolm S soon after I received the hat, getting the giving feeling. I wore the hat all around Mexico, and didn't lose it until two years afterwards, consider that in relation to people, consider all that I have lost for less tangible reasons than that that hat had to exist on my head. Anyway, that day I wore it and some far-out

Indian skirt; not a hustling costume at all, but just an expression of I don't give a fuck for we both are soon going to be dead anyway. So that is how I appeared to Tom O, the bondsman from Forth Worth. I didn't have much to say to him, already filled with disgust with reports of him from the F's. He was Texas on the hoof, appraised me immediately and told me to get my things together—that we were leaving for Ft. Worth in two hours. So I told him I didn't have any money, and he told me to meet him at his hotel in a couple of hours, just like that, shit, and I told him I need money to pick up my things in Nuevo Laredo so he gives me ten, and I make it to M for the baby double time, buying her a new pair of pink Mexican baby shoes on the way—a goodbye to Mexcity, Veracruz, and New Laredo. We dress in the *casa de huespedes* and go through customs which we had never even considered the whole time we were there, not ever having officially crossed. It is somehow illegal to live on the other side, especially if you are hustling. So I stop in with the baby to say goodbye to my friends at immigration, and I don't think they even checked us. No, for I had a bag of groceries or something, and certainly they knew us by then, only on the American side we checked in and I gave a special Mexican flourish—fuck you, Laredo border patrol of the streets and awful turnstile nickels and liquor tax, which I finally end up paying on an impulsive bottle of tequila.

At the hotel where I was supposed to make some scene with the bondsman I find Ray already out. I am numb, the height of the miracle does not extinguish the tragedy. Maybe this is the way Ray felt when he came out to Hoboken with me waiting for him pregnant and fucked in every direction; feeling that someone has made an enormous fool of you. This isn't the way it should be; I wonder what caused it:

extreme exhaustion, despair, I have never ever felt such despair as in Laredo. Even as leveled as it may seem in writing, I cannot help but come back to the human trying to tell what it is like to come back to life again without wanting to....

And then there is the baby Rachel, and Ray's physical presence. The first thing he wants on the street is a piece of chocolate cake. I am extremely self-conscious with him and we talk of the business. We are in the presence of the bondsman, this is meant to be just an interlude of legal delay until Ray is sent back to New Jersey. There is also a sheriff sitting in the front seat, the baby and Ray and me in the back. I am ashamed; it had something to do with that ten dollars, it had something to do with the dinner we were invited to along the road and had to say, well, of course we didn't have any money and he, big-hearted hospitality, bought us all steaks and bragged about the quality of the restaurant we were going to and joked with Ray and me and I didn't answer him and Ray protected me, but I think it made him sick, too. Ray is in control I discover later, and I am just a useless wife who was so tired out that I did not dare to enjoy anything anymore, the very dress that I wear is a badge and I know that everyone knows what I have been through to keep things going.

And Dallas is two connected inclinations with a big hotel in the middle and dark street night of nowhere at all and I sigh relief as we pass through, too much this proximity of death. The baby Rach sleeps next to us on the seat and I am unable to take care of her anymore. Say this is the end.

Hotel in Ft. Worth, paid for by the bondsman of course, who seems to take every opportunity to walk behind me and bug me, as if I had fucked him. The conscience of the whole world is digging my ass. Nancy F says later that this hotel is a center for hustlers, call girls, dope addicts, et cetera ... Another ripping cord to my neck muscles, how I am hoping to hold my head up in such a state? Tell the truth, unburden myself, and hope that people will stop directing it all back to me, unconsciously? Will that help? I have no trust in any but my own methods to protect myself and they are silence and contempt—so my eyes pierce Nancy F as she says this and I hold a permanent grudge probably.

Rachel slept on the floor and we arranged pornographic sessions of getting together again. Arranged? Pornographic? We have been married too many times under too many dubious circumstances, how does it do it to us?

Go back. We both immediately want to go back. My urge is to go back without delay and my first words to Ray when he is out of the Webb County Jail are that I would like to take him to Nuevo Laredo and show him what a real border town is like. I had done some research in the legal library to pass time and found that bail bond is good no matter where you go in the intervening time as long as you show up in court again on the specified date. But we have no money and we are both tired out, as I say, and besides, the bondsman wanted us nearby where we would be in sight of his risk. I am also conscious of our own risk having read that a bondsman can recall his bond anytime he thinks that the risk isn't worth it; since I can read this man's despicable character from his face and his name, I am sure that if an agent from New Jersey were to approach him with a deal he would betray us. I was afraid of another kidnap and maybe I talked Ray into it, or maybe we talked each other into it. I am glad to share the responsibilities again....

Ask why we got such a disreputable bondsman? It is hard to get someone to take on trust a border case because of exactly the schemes we ponder. Everything is well above board and we are off to meet our patrons to see what above board means to them. And we find that they love art—and that is where Ray comes in, being surely poetry's representative in the flesh. And they loved him, and they loved me, too, but I am too desperately frantic a picture of what poetry can do to the soul to be accepted easily. I have always been shy, maybe that shyness has always been an armor for the great darkness within me, truly matching in fact Ray's Neptunian depths. God, I want to make it all human somehow. Too much dark and light clashing, let me have an even cultivation of the seeds.

I had thought that it was my devotion, that my sacrifice in Mexico had kept us alive, and now in Texas it became clearly dependence on poetry, and poetry has lofty words to describe a purity I had a long time been on vacation from. So where was I to turn for sympathy? Maybe I should distill my own poetry so that I can find a correspondence (and don't think this isn't an enormous drive, look at this book!). I am extremely curious about what has happened to me, even to the point of wanting to sample it all again.

A simple life in Fort Worth, a couple of times I lounged beside a leisurely swimming pool, and divined in myself a quality beyond this mixture of share and exuberance, sense the presence of a growing pride; and when they offer us money to leave, when they offer through Ray this possibility of the baby being taken care of by some rich people where she will be safe, and I will not have the immediate worry that my investigations will be tampering with anyone else's life but my own.

MEXICAN MEMOIRS

In Fort Worth we couldn't even find a suitable place to score, and my thought now is that if I could have had some vision of the lotus blossoms' vibrations, I could have maintained more unity with Rachel's countenance. For she was conceived and grown in issue of marijuana, and coming away from it is infinitely worse than going to it. And I am still truly an emotional junkie, at this moment, but will not allow myself to be taken through changes in directions unnatural to my wont again. But that is what happened in Fort Worth. It was an exaggerated spread of nothing. Undoubtedly somewhere outside the city limits the red dirt grew soul we needed to distraction. Have you ever been so desperate that your own desperation prevented you from taking care of what was driving you to desperation? That is what I told the doctor the one time that I went for medical advice about a cure, and he told me that I was harboring an illusion—imagine that? So, Fort Worth, you make me sick! And I no longer apologize, but turn myself on in retrospect and regain what was lost, and I will, I *will*, as sure I am building up to another climax here, and you know what that means. I will make it yet.

Book Three
Mexico City and Rural Excursions: Losing Rachel

Sensationless nightmares—the word gets around that there is a beautiful blonde American baby who needs a home, that there is a chance that some vagabond criminal poet and his wife have an eye to flee the country and are looking for someone to take proper care of their offspring, and she is a sweet child; one look is enough to see that. So it is arranged that way: one last look for us, one last look for the baby Rachel. Think of it that way: I want everyone to concentrate on how Rachel feels, and get as far out mystical as you can imagine it, for that's how it is, think I don't know in my bones what she is like. Somehow separate rooms, I can change diapers as someone in the darkness around me signs a paper in red ink. The notary appears to Ray and me; I need Ray's arm around my shoulder to help me, Oh God, the notary asks me if I am in my right mind and my signing hand says yes, and he collects half of the world in his briefcase and leaves my life (forever?). I think I got drunk that night, I was often drunk, obliterating my tears in a whirl of falling, no more dreams of river's brinks; what need, only make for the nearest shore.

What matter that we turn to Mexico again, small steps of life proceed ahead of me, hoping in fact that it is only the scenic railway—we return to our cabin security of T.V. dinners and beer and a haphazard

Indian blanket to warm up the dream a little chilled from cocaine rages of numbness in the back of my head.

Do you see?

The crossways at dawn in Fort Worth. We hail a taxi on the street, always figuring a spontaneous retreat is the hardest to pick up, the flat lid suitcase basket our only weight, to it added as the only item of the past a Mexican baby dress of the baby Rachel. Taxi to the airport, buying tickets we find no problem, no cops await us, of course not, but Ray is looking over his shoulder digging the entranceway as the cat asks him his name for the plane reservation, he forgets incognito preparation and says it out true, and we decide not to give a fuck, but for the border on he was known as P.K., and I was a registered miss, something that has gone down in the record too many times already. One stop in San Antonio for breakfast. I hate Texas, we hit Brownsville, find time to stop and we are again six months back and crossing the border. . . .

Hey, baby, ain't it good here? Oh, goody, hello, Mexico, this is another life again. In Victoria, we rush to the smallest bus station in town figuring to take a real raunchy ride for the first lap just in case anyone should try to piece together pictures of our exit, we make it away in trails of dust, every half-blood in the bus stop, some with Texas boots, digging me from the back, I know. It is something different to walk alone after a baby in your arms for so long, but forget that quickly please (no, no) and let's have our red star or red sun, red omnibus of the dog trail away from Matamoros plaza of fried beans and revolted eggs. Discomfort is no object, the floor of the bus almost makes it above being a dirt one and we have thrown ourselves head first into the culture this time. . . .

MEXICAN MEMOIRS

In Victoria, I made the drugstore and we rent a plush tile room on the plaza of archway waterfalls, there is nothing but drugstores, movie houses, waterfalls, and chicken salad bus stops in Victoria, but I found earrings and a new pair of drawers and, after a shower, figuring our getaway had been made, I recline on the bed, nude, hot, encouraged by Ray. And encouraged by Ray's concentrated presence, I master dreams of high bed come-on, while he watches zonkec words dribble from the pages he is writing, a letter to the people who have Rachel, already, as struck dumb as I am still now. In some unguarded moment lost along the way he had said to me, soft, "I feel sick about the whole thing, baby." Yeah, me, too, Ray. He is writing a letter for us both which he finishes and comes to me, sneaky on the bed, I get it so good I begin to feel guilty ... I love you, Ray, it's all right, well, we play the doubles with them and giggle the glees again that we are getting it so good from each other always, always beyond them.

What we can do twice we can do many times, and the first toilet I visit on the bus trip became revolutionary in my eyes. We are really making it this time, now we are into something in which we have the head start of past experience. Though we have lost once badly, we are still playing, let's start another stand.

I guess I learned some things about men that I never even had a chance to learn before, not that I wanted to. Think back to Washington and how it was sweet to know Ray from the first, everything was satisfied, but as I say when you get older you have to twist your mind a little, or get it twisted by the law, as I have....

Mexico City, *distrito federal,* Mexico D.F., Mexcity, dome-topped rocknrolls the whole day from five in the morning or so building up to a crush at several points in the day. Cry me strawberries, or silent *fresas* arriving into town from mud-walled vicinities of barefoot Indians. I am in awe, eat as many strawberries as I can. God, it is the damp fresh morning and I am loose in the world, half of the time alone. Ray and I talked our fool heads off, analyze emotional vibrations between us, drink coffee arriving in Valles, in the bus stop plaza which rises high in the air and overlooks a neighboring hill. After going through an hour of a cops-and-robbers paranoia scene about a guy in a red Volkswagen who wears cowboy boots (F.B.I.?), we drink more coffee, catching glimpses from behind the restaurant curtains of the fuzz closing in. I ate strawberries, hoping that Ray is only having a malevolent hallucination, but knowing the possibilities also otherwise, the town does not seem friendly, we find three of the possible ten eating places in town just in this cat and mouse episode. But we both calm down in time and decided to investigate the river's other side. The river's edge is muddy, we have walked down ivy Grecian steps to get to the river, step the Egyptian prow of one of the ferry canoes, the driver is silent and does not speak; he collects 20 centavos. We move down the silent river, the world moves above in reflections, oh look up at the Mexico—oh sky! We walk to an appointed bankside tree and get horny with the quiet sun, damp grass, and willow hanging and I am for fucking right there, but Ray feels the Indian river wash girls peeking at us. We walk square roads through the grass hut village of deep green, and think of investigating the back road as a secret exit out of town should we need it, return and drink beers and play polka rocknroll in an individual grass-roof cantina, which has grass curtains to make it all private. A ten-year-old girl serves us *cervezas* and hardly giggles. The open space across the river is a vision of infinite variations of green, healthy clean barefoot, it rains, commotion, we worry the rain will get us busted, the Everly Brothers sing somewhere, in Valles. . . .

Oh, sing it rocknroll, Elvis Presley mesmerizes us with his presence in ice cream parlor jukeboxes, we rent a hotel, not far from the river, upstairs balcony room next to the trees, the bedstead supports my thanks to life for giving me back Ray, it thunderstorms, the trees breathe, Ray and I talk but I get so tired I keep flaking out in the midst of Ray's out-loud ruminations, he keeps waking me up, talking desperately of the trees, asking me the same questions. Bonnie, I want to be a tree, help me! And I tell him to be a tree, he must live like a tree, the human limits are only just that, so be a tree if you like.

Stoned, and the rain falls and I watch. Finally we get ourselves together, walk to the outskirts of town, cruising the streets for suspicious cars, and make it back sneaky to the hotel room and pull out for Mexcity.

Rivers everywhere, pulling out of their courses, we hit Tamazunchale, another river, Rio Moctezuma, we pass avoiding the temptation to stop, Jocala circles past like a northern Nebula, now it is small towns sifting by the way to Mexcity mountaintop nighttime stars, look, look the empty space of lakes dry-eyed approach to the foot of Popo.

We arrive in Mexico City at night, and rent a much-too-extravagant 100 peso room in the Hotel Majestic on the plaza of the Zocalo. It was a great room, and we figured the police would never think to look for us in such a place. Plaza Zocalo in Mexcity looks like Red Square, and I am glad, being a total revolutionary. I sew in our quiet hotel room and the next morning call P and tell him our new situation and ask him to come to the hotel (we both envision fucking him, before he arrives). . . .

P arrives morning time with a joint and we take off, to score maybe, to change to another hotel in Villa Guadalupe, way out of town, smoke lots of pot there, talk stories with P on the bed there, make it to P's house, too, listen to sides—Ornette, Ray Charles—and talk of Indian pyramids. P has been held at nighttime superstitious bay by nearby Teotihuacán pyramid of the sun and tells us of hidden spearheads . . . and shifts right from that story to tell us of the magic mushroom people in the hills (mountains) of Oaxaca, Seraphita's cult of complete control, tells us of turning on with them, and we get the address and particulars and decide to go there, jump around in excitement not knowing it was so possible to be free.

Pot smoke. Villa Guadalupe cooks its religious hot chocolate for Indian morning, huge cauldrons of it, and there are tiny pancakes one inch around stacked like coins everywhere. The morning flags are flying. This is one of the large market areas, but Indian, and there is often a devil dance going around noon, the Plaza Guadalupe enormous shuffling knees of penitents across, the dance becomes astronomical coming up to the ultimate fountain of the chapel and rose petals fall and Popocatépetl looks on across the lake eye, no reflection. God.

Like a swinging teenage party—we meet a young painter-sculptor at P's Rio Street apartment, bebopping heels waggling to Ray Charles, he dances so intensely you just hold your breath knowing something beautiful is happening, and he is laughing to himself as he dances, also makes great nude teenage collages to illustrate films of Ray Charles rocknroll. He and his young chick, she dances, too, visitors of Mexcity also and rent a high-ceilinged studio, with beautifully finished floors and construct art things full of marijuana, pretty conceptions of patterns and mirrors and gold tassel flashback. . . .

MEXICAN MEMOIRS

From Villa Guadalupe we travel to Guernavaca, south of Mexcity across fog high chill, and rent a room in casbah step hotel up the side of steep hills. Ray says he is going to write for a couple of days, and we are almost out of money, so I leave him, return one hour bus ride to Mexico City, contact Emanuel de la G and rendezvous with him one day, and stay over at his request and make it another day also, the same scene as before, his Mex-Indian chest swells the pride of his big cock, giving me a workout, I make an easy 1000 pesos that way and return to Guernavaca on the early morning bus, watching the roads for suspicious-looking police cars, almost expecting to be stopped and hauled from the bus. But no, cool morning. Ray sleeps, I climb gleeful the high steps to him, he has been lonely and inactive, but it is cool now for we are off on our mushroom visit (projected length, two months—actual length, ten days) and we both know it is going to be fun, paradise, in fact, to plan (pot high, of course) such a great adventure.

We traveled a day and a night to get up to the mountains. It appears only a fifty-mile drive by the map but the trip takes thirty hours, the bus seems to go too fast even at that, and each hundred-foot turn in the road threatened to be the end of the line. There were two bus drivers, and my attention focused on one of them. But why am I interested in people? Life is as it is, I am tired of smelly rules.

Mainstreet mushroom town runs along the side of the mountain, parallel streets are up or down the mountain, but not evident. Main Street is a dirt road, and the road we arrive on in the bus becomes Main Street, and the market is perched on a precipice which faces west. The morningtime market as we arrive offers no more welcome than any of the other inhabitants, no one curious about us, no one even notices except a little boy who came up and asked if we wanted to buy mushrooms and Ray said yes and found out where the one hotel in town was, at the east end of the village. The road runs level as it is confined in the village and starts going up and down again immediately as it gets past the hotel. We check in—the prices are very high and the conditions primitive; not that I mind, in fact, I grew to love it and would have liked to have stayed there forever. The wooden stairs of the hotel passed upwards connecting balconies that grew more rickety the higher they got. We were on the second floor. The door was fastened by a padlock, but immediately in the room we discovered many knotholes which would make the living communal.

It is a great thing to start out on a trip with enough money. We indulged in a new kind of tourism, and hunted out the most ideal places, every once and a while returning to the hub Mexcity—oh Mexico, time snake, where I have to exert myself to raise as much money as possible quickly so we can get away and be safe again. I found out later that this is a cycle many Mexican prostitutes do with their boyfriends: fierce work, extended vacations, though I know none who got so elemental as us. We grew not to fear too much running out of money at the end of the line, because hitchhiking was possible, but then anything had possibilities of fear; there are always the police around.

Huautla. You learn to say these names, learn to say them passing through; approach a town and there is the rumor of its name, and when you are through it, you have learned it, and it is usually beautiful, too. Ever find it hard to accept that a dream place exists, like the peyote church in Brooklyn? That's how I felt about Huautla, and forgot about Seraphita with the street score, figured that was more hip anyway, and as long as we had them, might as well start eating. I ate a lot, immediately, having great faith (all of these organic highs are religious, don't ask me chemical effects), and immediately the bright day hotel window draws sounds of saxophones, clarinets, flutes, and danzón drums of the Indian hillside road top. The music quickly begun stops, a few beats of a march, we rush to the balcony and see the band, it is rinky-dink dissembled, all sizes of men in white wrapped-on trousers unanimously blow one bagpipe chord strong which peters out into creative frills and tootles according to each man's inability to control the register. That's how jazz began—a happy, full-of-joy music that starts shyly and then jumps by the hotel road below, exactly rhythmed to the bounce of Indian foot parade going by, at that moment the most beautiful expressive music of love ever heard, and then we see what it means; a girl in a white dress, arm held by a man in extra-white shirt and wrap between the leg pants, actually defined by the joy on his face as the bridegroom. They are modest, they are beautiful, the band plays their regal hopped-up walk through town, a bebop Indian waltz. That was the first mushroom experience: everyone in that walk through town loved them who loved each other, and I thought I saw the bride look up at our balcony.

Another day dawns and I contemplate the sun moving, or the earth moving—relativities of shadow and light that make the window a half-creeping of brightness, the rest still the blue birth of dawn, early in the morning. There comes to my head sad musics of a saxophone contemplating (musing) and in all the mountain heights I am puzzled where such a sound is coming from. I rouse Ray and we decide it comes from the graveyard down the road; it trails a cleft of greenness in the mountainside. This is the first truly pastoral music I have heard in my life, and it sings the blues, many mornings in Huautla, someone singing dawn to those already gone, such dedication of individual emotion, this blue and beautiful music, the mushrooms start to tell me something of life: whole other conception of living, again.

And when you take a shower in the morning there, in the wooden shower house it is cold, icy mountain stream water piped into a shower that is an experience itself if you can take it. I dig the torture, immerse myself in the ice cold and get reborn to sanity.

I still wear some of my Laredo dresses. When we packed up and left Texas, we sorted things out again. Every time we made one of these stops in time, we collected households of possessions and clothes, and then would clear out with only a basket and necessities again. We have battlements of household possessions all over the American continent's southern parts.

Huautla made me know that we were no more than tourists, really. So distant from the Indians, we were not able to talk to anyone. Most of the people seldom speak Spanish there anyway, this is an Indian village, the Catholic church at the other end of town is revered but that makes it no less Indian. We turn to each other our conversations, and I feel inadequate, answering Ray's probing of nature. He wants certainty to reply and I can give him no more than opinion. I am content in Huautla that there is no other source of information and that even if I do not answer well the conversation will be between us alone. Ray raises his head above the thin ageless blankets, the sun has made it completely through the window inconsiderate onto his head, like my shower a forceful awakening. We descend to the restaurant below. The kitchen hands are an old woman stirring over an immense pot hung over charcoals on the floor, an overdeveloped thirteen-year-old chick who is big, boisterous, and stupid. She serves the tables and cannot ever hold back her giggles, concentrates when we order eggs, beans, and bread and then repeats back to us what we have said, making a big thing of it and then has to be told all over again, repeats again, finally gets it straight, hops with comprehension, and lands with conviction on her overdeveloped feet and goes to talk to the woman, old woman serene over her pot and we pay no more attention to her for quite a while. This gives us a chance to view the rest of the kitchen setup: a little Indian boy who suffers indignations from the women, a big ole cat who prowls and perches and parades through the kitchen, an immense mongrel dog who knows he is not welcome and forks his nose around the corner of the entrance door cautiously looking for loot, centers his attention on an old lady, a healthy robust old lady who travels Mexico doing research behind her beribboned glasses, knows everyone too well for comfort, speaks Indian probably but just the same cannot suppress her unpleasant American accent in ordering breakfast (we think she is the fuzz). The dog is her friend, they are both old timers, and she has saved him pieces of her breakfast beefsteak and there is no alternative—to the management's dismay. The dog slinks around the wall side and nuzzles up his mug to her hand, she is so kind to it, and after he has finished there he makes it around to the rest of the tables bold and disreputable and gets bread pieces until his welcome is worn, and the monster teenage chick chases him out gyrating enormous fiestas of arm swing and calling him ancient names of insult, fetches a rock, and sends him away with the well-known motion of her arm. The little kid gets enthusiastic and follows the dog outside to throw more rocks, and when he tires of it the old dog's snoot sings mournfully across the window rock flowerbeds of ascending sun mountain morning, as we eat our breakfast. A truck driver inscrutably drinks morning beer with some specialty of the house he is eating. The chick who owns the hotel has a monopoly on the town, she owns the bus line to the outer world, the hotel which is a rickety tourist haven, one of a kind in Huautla, only one other restaurant in town, and it appears she handles all shipping of Coca-Cola and other regular commodities hauled by truck from the outside, probably rice and beans, too, so the truck driver is a little king, part of the management.

As surely as this hill-ground belongs to the Indian (though he has to buy beans and rice and Coca-Cola from the outside, magazines, newspapers, and movies) our life is our own; if we don't have that, what have we got? We walk up sides of adjoining mountains, searching through meadow grasses to find fresh mushrooms growing. They have to grow somewhere. We find lofty peaks which are like the sky itself, and the meadow field slopes downward looking gentle. I decide to go for a run and find myself speeding down the mountainside, unable to stop; God, let down your hand to give me some security of flight.

And we walk circles of dirt road ambush and pass Indians pitter-pat on the road with things on their heads wrapped in rags, and it is no shame, they don't even look at us. I am overawed. We walk for hours passing homes, passing women sitting outside, passing groups of unseen houses that form a tiny community, and no one says a word. So we ascend to a grove on top of another hill, its solitude unseen, but we discover fences and the exploration becomes less joyful. The grove's solitude beckons to me, but Ray resists, thinking of isolated tombstones and we sit, next to the fence, sit flat down on that

MEXICAN MEMOIRS

mountain road and feel small in the world of yellow, green, and blue. I start feeling horny in the sun and suddenly, though quiet, two lovers emerge nearby from under the fence and walk away, saying nothing. Coffee bushes grow on the side of the hill. A jeep mysterious with passengers passes quickly and pays us no attention. We find a neat solid cement bridge connecting a road's turn, a depleted mountain stream splashes down rocks to the edge of the road. It gets a hold of itself and goes under the bridge, which is dedicated to a Mexican president.

The mushrooms look like mushrooms... We bought a kilo (about two pounds) for eighty pesos (about six dollars), a shoebox full; they are dried to brown-black witheredness. Big and small, their thin heads project from the center like dried flowers, but more organic, brownish black, they look like the earth itself, and we spend a couple of hours tearing the stems off and throwing them away; I eat as I work. Ray is timid of them (too organic) but eats enough to get high. I go crazy and eat about a pound of them while we are in Huautla, knowing that I will worship the effects, the taste is something to be ignored, I keep eating, every time we return to the room I eat mushrooms. I ate so many mushrooms I was never able to describe or remember the immediate feeling of their effect coming on, but know looking back that I was high for months (this is the way peyote hit me, too—I can say a few beautiful high experiences, but the effect is a large time cycle change of life: how I get my religions) and the stomach gurgles in digesting these rinds of pure clean hilltop earth. We decide to eat something civilized to camouflage the stomach's toil; call the silly girl (she is the only one who didn't have any dignity) to our room and tell her we want tacos delivered to us in afternoon rooms of sensual enjoyment. A half hour later she brings us great tacos, hot, no salt, she has forgotten the salt and we do not taunt her ignorance, thinking it useless.

THERE IS SALVATION. I wrote it on the ceiling once, not even my own wall. . . . But it was legitimate, I mean sincere, and spontaneous, and I will explain: It was in New York City in the summer of 1959, late in August. Ray and I had already been to San Francisco and had a couple of dried peyote buttons which Wally dug out of some abandoned satchel in his cellar. There Ray had threatened my sight with the paintbrush shadowed in blue light as we were talking of life side-by-side on the bed in the stark white front room. The view of all else vanished, even daisy fields on blue I draped images of on the floor disappeared . . . and in New York one month later we had borrowed a top floor apartment for a night and asked for privacy to adventure a full dose of fresh peyote and after we gagged it down and our stomachs were churning madly to turn into nourishment this strange vegetable cactus, my foot started patting immediately in unseen patterns of rhythm (though I was merely nervous anticipating, and that's not far from true anyway, these momentous highs. Ray went out to buy us hamburgers to add to digestion. I am thrown into a void, try to distinguish his figure departing the doorway seven stories down to the street, checking which way he goes. I am not sure, but I think I see him digging a chick passing. He talks to her and they walk together, and I retire to my thoughts. The loneliness is not healthy being so induced, and I always felt unwanted when Ray went out alone. And my foot pats became more insistent. I realize that my foot is alien to normal control. It is expressing something I do not comprehend. Up tempo; I try to concentrate on the sound of my foot and discover that it is a violent agitation, angry element of force, dancing, clacking fury. I look down in curiosity and before the sight of my feet I see my hand flexing, fingers and fist with scissors expertly eating up the air's planes. It was the scissors, whipping the air and pouncing on each blade the other, syncopating each passionate foot sound, ashamed (knowing that I am letting loose anger at Ray for leaving me, frustrated because I long for him to be with me at every moment, and do not want to spoil moments by crying that he leaves, but I hadn't realized that I was roused to such a pitch) I force myself to stop. (I reason to myself: Ray is trying to do something nice for me, better, something nice for us together, and when he returned, all the time in between will be consummated by being together again, giving to each other new scores of conception come upon meanwhile). At this point, silent, I know that I am high, that I have just gotten a "rush," I will tell Ray (about the scissors?) . . . with a sense of accomplishment, I lie on the mattress on the floor, my weight feels good coupled with the bed enclosing the insecurity of my stomach and the candle at my head on the floor will make a nice picture for Ray when he arrives. Till then I muse, my eyes slowly grasp the candle and focus the luminous upper wax, not even grown warm yet, it glows waiting the flame, the destruction travels downward, the flame aspiring upwards. What is reality, where the means to grasp this, the flame's even power is fed by gases from the core of action, the wax sapping upwards the rooted wick, the wick, look at the wick, it is a monk with his head bowed in prayer, the huge dignity of him upright standing in the middle of it, giving of himself, and allowing that he be the means of connecting everything with everything. No, it is just a piece of cord, dead, destroyed, nothing human even when it was new and fresh, now charred, all its visible existence in flame, its utmost attainment the end crust, the bowed head, the twine taking on a new form and cumulative shape, what has survived of its previous lengths, glows, goes up in smoke. . . .

And I grabbed up the candle quick and wrote on the ceiling THERE IS SALVATION, for the candle, the wick, the monk, Ray. . . .

Ray returned soon with the hamburgers and claimed that later in the night I threatened him with scissors.

. . . That is what is known as seeing the light, and it is probably corny to talk about it as a great comprehension, probably telling too much of the truth when I say that this was one of my life's great religious manifestations. I had known a lot of despair before that time, and a lot of fear since Ray and I had married (the time Ray and I were groping up the unlighted stairs of a friend's house in D.C. and Ray stopped and turned on me and I stepped up into him and screamed and screamed and saw myself from the outside and cried and couldn't stop, till Ray got fed up and wouldn't comfort me anymore) silly fear, and now began to sense that there was a reason for the fear and actually *saw the light*, knew that there was salvation before I comprehended the fear. And I remembered this many times in the next months, the long peyote high working from that time, that salvation is an omnipresent thing, just like the void—and I steal a secret out of time here. . . .

So we figured we had been set off to a good start, I mean that the trip away was finished; for one thing the money was running out and it was time to think of going back. The hotel had been very expensive, the monopoly making it so and the assurance of tourist trade making it into town. One half of the people I know who have gone to Mexico have made the thirty-hour trip up into the mountains to get to Huautla, everyone knows about it. Course there are other places to get mushrooms, we look across valleys to nearby hillside towns and think to make the footpath trip and check, check the hillsides themselves for growth, see flowers, even ask the possibilities of renting houses. The comprehension that the money is gone is quick, we pack up the rest of the mushrooms and what we carry of less importance, and get our bus tickets the next morning. Blue sky and cold water, I don't want to say goodbye, hey, Ray, I want to live in salvation forever. Yes, but we have to get out now, baby, can't get stuck here for it is too dangerous. And we kind of get mad at the proprietress when she gives us the bill. A lady on the street sees a new light in my eyes and takes me to her house to look at native Oaxacan dresses for sale—a beautiful costume brown shirt with enormous yellow sun broadside on the breast, but we have no money, so I just look.

We sit on the bus in the morning sun moving down the hillsides, we are maybe just scared, I want to clutch Huautla and take it—a concentration—in my hand. The driver becomes unofficial and makes a special stop down hill streets to pick up the lady tourist, and back up to the regular road in town, which also goes out of town past the market. Finally, we start, but then stop across the street from the market brink of the blue sky and sit there doing nothing for half an hour which so upsets me on top of the emotion that I start to draw. I wanted to draw an impression to take with me forever, and found it simple, though hard to do what you want to do, it is fun to ignore what you want to do and do what you can, which you discover was really what you wanted all along anyway. I drew a funny cartoon cactus, as skillfully as I could, and Indian men whose asses I dug in the market, and incorporated their wraparound pants and huge cactuses against the sky, hill brink not indicated other than miles away scenery, so a blank view, the hidden precipice—and the bus starts as I scribble happily the last of it.

And this will save me from the boredom brought on by the realities you know you just don't want to be bugged by anyway. This is how I feel at going back to Mexico City, but there is music, and pot, and I can draw now, I can spend hours of just seeing things the way I want to and recording the best I can on paper. I draw a vine and tree-lady for Ray after we have left the bus and are hitchhiking along the deserted plain, conversation which brings the elements up so clear to him (me, too, I'm doing most of the talking) that he doesn't know whether to be scared or just dig it. We sit under a tree and watch road workers, and finally, amazingly, get a ride. It is two Italians who call themselves brothers; they ask us where we have been, we point up to Huautla, I try to keep Ray from talking about the mushrooms, but he is drawn into it. Ray opens the package showing mushrooms to the traveling brothers, and they are almost as fast turning on us with an exhibit of their handkerchief full. And they hadn't even been there lately, we knew, we were. So it all ended happily and they gave us a big lecture about not taking the mushrooms back to the States. A moral come-on about it, in fact, and we say oh no. Ray, in fact, gives most of them away in Mexico City, to my dismay; I could have done in the whole kilo. . . .We check into a hotel in Tehuacán and I start drawing Van Gogh chairs, tilted rooms, shadows of cat ghosts in the mirror. Ray metamorphosed into a sitting-in-drawers portrait done from memory.

So I was eating frantically, wanting to finish the mushrooms myself. Ray and I sit in candlelight just looking at how beautiful even an impersonal hotel room can be. We decided to hitchhike early for we really didn't want to hitchhike at all but figured it would be cool on unpopulated roads (we remembered U.S. hitchhiking busts where nothing had happened because there was nothing wrong, but now it was different). I thought we were completely out of money but in Tehuacán Ray comes up with money he has stashed and with that we get a hotel and bus tickets to Mexcity—

. . . . .

—Mexcity

The air feels hot on my arms. I am riding cross city, Reforma, Insurgentes, toward the University city campus by bus, whirling the high hot afternoon corners. I am on my way to J's whorehouse for the first time. I am to meet my first date arranged by J—in the hot afternoon behind drapes she is doing her fingernails. Her hard red hair disconcerts me. A card-playing whore, she and her friends pass afternoons (I will later pull a knife on her pimp, my outlaw scene, trying to get the money and succeeding) playing cards; they are playing cards as I come in and my john rises to identify himself as I come in, he is very blonde, and seems entranced. After I chit-chat with J, we kiss in front of her and get sent into the back room so we can be alone. . . .

And I lay across the bed playing, there is not much to do but that. And in fact there isn't, he keeps making a funny noise in his throat and asking me why I am so beautiful in a pleading tone, and taking off his wristwatch, he starts to play around. He does all the action, and it is a hot afternoon and all I am thinking of is myself, within reason, got to get the money, but it is natural pleasure and this cat is O.K., and I think of J and the others sitting outside, and the cat is going down on me, and I am trying to get him off of me cause I just want to fuck and get it over with, and I'm afraid if I get too involved I will get burned somehow. But he is going down on me and exciting me and I am not able to get him to fuck for a long time while we struggle and finally he gets close up and I grab him and put it in, getting what I want, and also supposedly him, and everything turns out O.K. and everybody is happy, he keeps asking me why am I so beautiful. He speaks English and wears a slick mustache, makes it to J's about once a week, but I am set up earlier for three hundred pesos. We all speak, after we clean up, and take our goodbyes because this cat has to get home or something, and I go back to the hotel....

It's hard to figure why I do well as a whore in Mexico City. I am usually shy of people, but I become such an ardent hustler that as the money accumulates I grow proud. Ray required pornographic schemes when I got back to the hotel to satisfy his curiosity.

We didn't want to hitchhike ever, really. It was too dangerous, but after a while memories fade a little (especially memories of the law) and we became just so, all the time caught up in what we were doing ... Every trip we took away from Mexcity (and we both went through a regular set of changes which made it necessary for us to get away, especially me, and I was driven to complain to Ray of what I feel is killing me: hustling. And I always get so depressed about the whole thing that after two or three weeks in Mexcity I start getting sick) we started out with a good sum of money and headed back broke and hungry, trying to stay away as long as we could feel safe, even without money; the beach at Salina Cruz, where we forfeited shelter and food, thankful for the warmth from west sea wind chill of night. Wandering cows and dark shadowed horses came to be friends with me. We dread the heat of day, our lips crack, no water, we try to hide from the sun under a prickly tree bush, but the lizards resent our disturbance. I take all my clothes off to avoid all but the breeze which occasionally saves us; we didn't know that we had come to a desert climate. God, nature's crust crudely burnished. But I don't want to go back to Mexcity. I am probably more insane than not.

Last night I dreamed that I was hungry; a pack of matches was the only thing available. I bit into the cover and found it not like food at all. I tried to tear the matches out with my teeth, trying to make the matchbook cover palatable, and realize it is useless, put it aside. I am reminded in the morning sun by matches scattered on the floor . . . I am as shocked at myself as anyone might be.

I can hardly believe that what I write is me. So it's all confusing if you stop to think about it seriously—better to make it a game, maybe even revel in it.

Sometimes I wonder what people think; not people reading this, but people who saw us in that time. Usually I start out thinking of the general beauty of the things we undertake, the satisfaction of being able to draw, reworking conversations we have had with friends, or interesting conversations I have had with johns (Ray now calling them "fish") and then from that I start considering, though briefly, what the other participants feel. But I usually prefer to have faith in what we personally have done, said, and felt, and if the opposite reaction was not good, then it is they who have missed out, somehow. . . .

This is Dome City. I have no idea of time. My address book fills with slips of paper and calling cards which will never be used. The chick ("The Chick") has come to clean our room while we are out to breakfast. I sit on the toilet thinking of reasons not to think about it: the day's usefulness will determine how soon we can get out of town, but there are present considerations, and I get horny waiting for Ray to come back. I wash out all my drawers as a security measure and admire them as they lay colorfully sodden on the bathroom floor, where I display them to dry.

Ray decides when he gets back that I look so good I ought to walk out and try to sell it. I walk out, but don't try to sell it, wander streets looking up, senselessly waiting for some vision, trying to force a vision, and when I get back there is a conclave of new arrivals in the hotel room who sit around friendly while I put them down, high on pot.

I draw sights from my imagination, memories: on Ninth Avenue and 43rd Street there is a bar across from the Seven Arts coffee shop; you go back and forth across Ninth Avenue depending on whether you want beer or coffee. I met Jack D there and he asked Ray out loud in front of me if he could scoff my box, and I get insulted but can't say anything for we are newly married and Ray is in authority, phenomen-authority. Turn time on and get to New Jersey, any Sunday saw me looking forlorn, calling Orpheus from the sky over Rahway Prison, the canal bridge, exposing a very undesirable riverbed, graveyard stink, jail-yard pasture smell, the walls hold it all in. Ray works in the stockroom where they bug him with fiscal inventories just as if it were exactly real.

"So I suppose you're very bitter," a chick giving me an interview for a job says, or, "Oh, I am sick of people being mad," a new return to the city from far away says. Being bitter is a means of holding your head up when you are too low for anything else to help; then usually, if you have any heart, you can build things up from there . . . And I hate the ones that get next to you, acting sympathetic, and then tear you apart from the inside out.

I was introduced to another house, in the Rio section of Mexcity. All Mexcity is split into little groups of streets with connecting avenues, like the American tourist section streets of continental cities, or back town *barrios* of revolutionary presidents. This section near where P lived was all names of rivers of the world. The house was very quiet, an afternoon appointment with a cat who sat and talked for about ten minutes. I admire his wristwatch. Noticing the time, he suggests that we get it over with; this was one of those previews to the house where I fuck one of the regulars as a test, and I didn't like him much. He was attuned to some kind of social come-on I couldn't discern, but he was obligated to make it once so we did and he hung around too long for my likes; he was a small faggish forty-year-old who was up on some social hip I didn't understand. He kept trying to get the informational goods on me, for the glory of the house, but I remain tight-lipped, and unimpressed. The madam shoos him out finally and enters with a young bonus for me who must have just dropped by, a thirty-year-old good-looking Spanish blondish suntanned man who had no real business there, I figured, but did him and it was a healthy pleasure after the kind of off-handedness of the previous one. I figured I was lucky to do so well when I didn't even like the place and suspected that it didn't like me either. I preferred to wear my revolutionary get-up rather than their normal respectable good looks that bored me because of their dishonesty. And later this chick sends me out of town to a party at a rich man's house and I snubbed them all and was sent home and had to pay for the cabs myself.

I walk the streets at night hopeful. Ray stays home to answer the telephone, I am getting sicker with the Mexcity constant chill and damp, nerves grating.

Ray had been writing and hanging out with young students in the hotel; he decided he wanted me to make the scene with one of them while he watches, so I seduce a young kid, talking to him of our intention as I move closer to him on the bed, clad in panties and bra as usual, high on pot, put my hand on his leg and sit next to him, and it was a whole amateur high school come-on bit, slow and tantalizing, while Ray watched, and when we finished making it, Ray writing notes and digging from various angles of the room removes his clothes, and says, "don't start to cool off yet, baby, I'm next." And Ray and I fuck in all the rubble.

I get upset, decide I had liked fucking for pleasure, got horny one day and went down to the kid's room and fucked him again, and got comforted to boot, because he felt sorry for the way I had to live. Man, it really broke me up, in fact I got sick of it, and when I returned to the hotel room, O.K., straight, Ray was waiting like a fury to punish me for what I did.

Tilty buildings I look out the windows to, and draw, panes and all, Ray threatens to leave me, and I threaten to leave him if the violence continues. He maintains it is good for a chick to get pounded on once in a while for it increases the circulation and makes her pretty. I am brought back to our meeting in Washington, D.C.; we fucked a lot the first time, all night and all day. Ray also says that fucking is good for chicks: the more they fuck, the better they look and are, and later when he went to jail I figured I should uphold his views and fucked everyone in sight, from the first night to the last.

I am lazy and stubborn; most of the time I think about fucking or about doing something that will excite my senses. Ray takes off to Tehuacán in the state of Puebla, to wait for me till I raise sufficient money for us to make a complete trip. He takes most of the money I have got so far, says he will travel to Veracruz while he is waiting for me. I will have to pay the hotel bill and stay there till I do good enough to join him in Tehuacán. . . . It took four days for me to get the money. I was really bugged, thought Ray was turning cold on me in weird ways. I was lonely, but wanted to get out of Mexcity, too, and maybe this was the surest way to get out quick.

When I met Ray days later in Tehuacán (didn't I want to go to Veracruz, too? but that would be too conspicuous) he had a red bikini for a present for me to wear to the beaches, and books of French prose to excite my senses. We make up in the hotel room, digging the outsides through shutters, hardly remembering the room we stayed in around the corner, mushroom trails heading off in other directions. We are introspective; Ray knows he is trapped with me.

The day months before in Veracruz when we met Zack R, the peyote man, and his red-headed, red-skinned, orange girlfriend, his beard or something scared Rachel into whoops of shyness she never felt before, and she cried, inconsolable, and she cried that way every time she saw him till everyone thought it was some prophecy. The red-orange girl flips out on pot fumes she inhaled and ran out (maybe feeling something too big to dare expression of) and Ray and Zack run out to keep track of and help her, we don't see them for a couple of days, the chick got away and retired to her meditations (she wanted to be a nun). Funny, in the afternoon we had tried to turn them on to music, sitting in the doorway, Rachel cried the whole time they were there to visit.

I am an evil woman. When Ray was in jail, just after our marriage —we had been married six months—he kept asking me when I was going to fuck someone else. At the three-month point, or before, he had fucked other chicks. I had halfway expected it, but didn't know how to act, trying to hold my heart together, making decisions how to act. I didn't fuck anyone, though I looked around and considered it, feeling left out, too, until the night that Ray hit the Hudson County jail. We figure that I fucked fifteen people in the period Ray was away. See what I mean about hot life?

What are these legends growing in my head? All of it is about to fall out completely on the page....

What is all this nervousness and sun shining in the window—me, in my new bikini lolling around by the windowsill. The grand old stucco building with beautiful balconies that people put to use, everything you see in Mexico is alive. This Tehuacán morning I come onto Ray in my new bikini, O.K., Ray, it is time to straighten everything out, I am ready, no reason not to. My head is twisted in pain, even good things move me to tears, get me close enough to Ray that I can cry it all out, or forget it.

The piles of fish stink up the ends of beach. Late morning vultures are getting drunk eating so many abandoned fish. Everyone stays clear of that section of the beach where vultures make big fools of their goofy selves, eating too much rotten fish, staggering around the beach, big black clowns doing a dance, and if I made it there later in the day, the fish were all eaten up, only the smell on the sand and huge designs of big birds' feet remaining.

To go to Coatzacoalcos we took a bus through Veracruz. The bus drives by Villa Del Mar, we touch the sea at Mocambo, see the long walk up the beach where we swam with no clothes.

Through Alvarez and across the ferry, before that across the bridge at Boca del Rio, fishing village black with vultures, beads on the ferry at Alvarez, onto solid ground again, the rushes of the river past, another four hours and we arrive in Coatzacoalcos evening time—hot, the water nearby, the bus lets us off one block from the portwall market section, it has started to rain. In a hotel room with shutters, we get high, hole up there, the sound of the sea furious sometimes. The joint down the street is open, its corrugated sliding walls rolled up. The place emits light and sound as we approach to get our coffee, and people look at us, and it doesn't bother me.

Funnytime big iron bed, the whole place looks very rustic but has an air of American organization about it, I am bugged because of the rain, and Ray wants to get out of there quickly, as it is too expensive.

I want to look at the sea. The water is always beyond us, not seen for the hills, and walking down in the easiest direction we arrive at the market, quickly pick out a hotel, one block from the portwall water, move from the yellow hotel we found. Our new hotel is pink and has a curlicue colonial cornice in front, over which is our room, with two flimsy mattresses and iron underneath which threatens of bugs. But we move anyway and go direct to the nearest bus as soon as I can get dressed and swallow some pills to speed me faster to the sea, gulf of Coatzacoalcos. The bus moves from the port along the sea wall picking up visions of house yards, vultures in the river at the right, turns left, and some dune sand immediately announces the change of roads. The sand slips under us ponderously, and then up and down huge dunes a half mile in circumference in which valleys of little valleys form and there are houses and properties and dogs and Coca-Cola signs. We sit on the crowded bus excited—the sea has shown a little from the bus so we immediately get off and jump in.

And the next day we moved to even another hotel in Coatzacoalcos. Our fears were growing, the money was almost gone, already, we moved to a wood slat hotel perched in the air, actually over the market though the shape was more makeshift than that of a building. The balcony had such a slope in its boards from individual footsteps that we kept as close to the wall as possible, more rustic this hotel than the one in Huautla—almost immediately we are out of money and know that we are in trouble and plan ways to cut out in safety.

And we fought a lot—pressures rising—I was convinced that Ray was losing interest in me. The only times it seems otherwise is when we are fighting, and I get very scared at the violence, especially in this rickety hotel over the market where everyone can hear. The main scene at this hotel was one of us sitting in the room (the heat unventilated, the bed naked, boards seeping heat, trying to cool it and wait for the other to get back from a rampage walkout—too mad to tolerate the company anymore.

Sadness to fight about money, or scenes, like the day we went to the beach and immediately got into such a fight on top of a huge dune approaching the sea, dogs barking around us, we were screaming at each other, unable to cope with the fury. I wanted to stop it in any way and shouted at Ray to go away and get out of my life, told him to beat it, or similar uncouthness—which he cannot stand in me knowing I use it to put down people on the street. Uncontained, angry, he went and I wanted to pursue him immediately and take it back, but he disappeared over the dune. I sat crying and cooled off, then got up and wandered, my head disarranged by tears, people stared at me over the dunes as I walked to the water. I am a tragic figure searching for him for an hour, my fears pictured him hiding behind the next hills taunting me. I return to the hotel in Coatzacoalcos, the rickety afternoon waiting, the hot sun shines smack again, the balcony facing the port, and sit and wait for him there and when he gets back we slowly make up. (NYC 1960, Ray had been interested in Marlene because of her suicidal tendencies; I had introduced them. I met her when I was hanging around fucking the same group of useless big band musicians she was, and I had tried to comfort her, thinking her more far out than I. She felt a personal grief about each relationship; even with the ugliest it was love—and then even after Ray fucked her she stayed at our house ironing her clothes, washing her hair and using my comb, would come sit and talk to me in the kitchen while I walked the baby crying at night, and elucidated to me the reasons she could be called suicidal, her pregnancy by this cat we mutually fucked. But she had loved him, and chased him, where I just copped his keys and made off with his records, due payment for my kindness, and mourned the loss of his baby, my God, all that for such a rat. I cannot help but sympathize, and understand Ray's interest, and he continues to fuck her over my wild objections, and threatens to leave me and go with her if I complain—and that put me in my place, I meekly follow him around, carrying Rachel in my arms, asking Marlene how long ago he started for home. She invites me into her room, the bed where they fuck, asks me admiring questions about him, and the baby, and our love together; I hate her.)

I struggled every bit of the way with reasons why I shouldn't fuck other people. Mainly because I want to remain close to Ray, partly to preserve myself, my drawing, and inspiration, but I was finally convinced that the reasons to fuck were greater. And besides Ray had a lot of time to be involved in other thoughts—and I found that he got tired of consoling me for my hard lot. It was straight action, either I was out hustling, busy, or we were spending the money and then went out again, and everything that was not business was supposed to be pleasure, sacred, necessary, but the moment any irritation comes up between us the whole story comes out in very personal glyphs and the arguments take longer and longer and it gets so that we both can't even stand to enter the argument anymore knowing the enormity of involvement beforehand, and begin to concentrate it. (I tell Ray to "beat it" or "get off my back.")

My one recollection of a scene on the beach that was nearly normal was lying with my legs stretched to the westward sun, in soft sand, entertaining a huge illusion that I was getting fucked by the sun. This was supposed to be an act I was putting on for Ray, but I know all along that it is serious, not only do I feel I get fucked by the sun, but feel obligated to be sincere in my squirmings of lustfulness, my bikini marks the sand in exact points of sensual plot. Ray is sitting next to me talking in a low drone about how he is getting excited, and I sometimes wonder if he is sincere, too, and we fuck there in the sand, and it is wild and elemental, and a successful scene I would think.

He is unsatisfied and we leave Coatzacoalcos in the afternoon, half of our possessions behind in the abandoned hotel room. We had gone out looking as though we were going to the beach, the most precious things in bags, but we had so little it really hurt to lose half: a bunch of de Sade books, one of my bikinis, clothes. We don't carry manuscripts any more, all that left behind in Texas.

Hitchhiking at forks in the road just beyond town, an open-backed truck takes us twenty-five miles across the isthmus. We had decided not to go back through Veracruz, so we have to cross Mexico at the skinny part then go back up through central Oaxaca to Mexcity.

We catch a ride with a salesman who has to stop off the road at Mateo after two hours, and eat eggs on the guy's money while he takes care of business. I wonder if I am going to get sold in the bargain, the town frolics in its Indian way as we quietly eat, both still bugged. I pulled the emergency cord and exited us from Coatzacoalcos, now we are wandering, no money, the only object to get back to Mexcity but it is no better there, it all resides within our heads. And Ray plays music on the jukebox and we enjoy it for a couple of minutes—hey, never put down music.

We do at some point along the way get so that we can talk again, the hurt stops and we look forward to getting back to Mexico City and promise each other the music and pot. Dig the scene on the road—the warm air we could sleep out in, the car lights coming, we panic, not knowing whether we are in the middle of the road or at the side, unable to see. No cars coming north, so we take one going back, double back through Tehuantepec hoping to get a ride in town, under the starry night, a bank of lights around the town and walk through unseen in the darkness, songs coming out lighted soft windows, the man who dropped us in Tehuantepec picks us up again and buys us bus tickets....

There are no towns near by Tehuantepec, desert surrounding, the sea blows strange winds across the hot atmosphere which with absence of civilization makes the sky black and clear for all the stars to shine through—the only normal-sized town nearby is Oaxaca, one hundred miles, and we travel the night by bus. Perch up on some highway mountain pulled off the road in the early hours of day for the bus driver to sleep, but it is extremely cold for us and we get out and walk around, walk back into bushes but it is still too dark and scary.

Into Oaxaca city as the sun comes up, into a place that has been open all night with beer drinkers and just now cleaning out the vomit and shit on the floors, bad nightmare of filthy dance hall, the stage is an obscenity from which the musicians are still retiring and we want to get something to eat and do in spite of the smell, and the food was bad, too, and they could not understand why we want to eat after such a hot night. The Oaxaca morning gets hot very fast and we get into an argument about which is the way out of town, I always feel my sense of direction is infallible.

Draw me the Oaxaca morning as we pass through pink gold green sandstone hill and the driver of the truck is telling us about gold in them hills. The town nearby where we stop for eggs (the truck driver with no hesitation bought us breakfast, sometimes I really love people) is named Pueblo de Oro, or something wildly fantastic like that, like making everything a true story—and we eat eggs and Ray flirts with the waitress. Swirl! The sun coming up over everything we drive madly in the truck and the two drivers are so courteous to us that one of them insists on riding outside on the dashboard so that Ray and I can sit together, in the cabin. We approach sandstone hills swirling up and up the roads till we reach a huge place with the beginnings of mountain ranges on all sides, elemental. From a special particular spot on this place you can see three volcanoes at once in the sky, white with snow against the yellow and green surrounding fields. And where the mountains that form the basin of Mexcity start, the hill is purple rock all creviced upward. You see what immensities of bottom structure make mountains! Orizaba hangs on the side of a hill, all overgrown with gardenias, water ducts, canals, and abundance of green in such lushness as I have never seen before, and keep twisting your head this way and that because you can hardly believe that such beauties exist all at once to your eye—and when it starts to go out of view you are impressed with the injustice of having to leave such a sight behind—(when the sun hits the ice and snow of these mountains first thing in the morning and blood runs down the crevices for an hour it is a show of unbelievable image that you don't care to describe anyway, horror or beauty, you just are struck with your eye stuck there on it and can't stop looking till the show is over)....

And Ray and I sit side by side, the truck driver's hand threatens to grope me, but doesn't, time leaves things behind and promises more to come....

Truck ride takes us through Puebla, around to the east of the Mex-city basin and then directly in from the east as if from Veracruz. In Puebla we have a lot of trouble keeping up with each other, spent almost a whole afternoon, irritable and tired. I am holding the cigarettes, and Ray asked for one and for some reason he intended for me to light him one or something, and I was already offended by something else and just held my hand out with the cigarette pack in it till he almost reached out to get it and then dropped it to the ground— I can't remember the brand of cigarettes but I know it had a red and white striped pack; Mexican cigarette packages are gaudily striking anyway, with funny names. So Ray got just as unreasonably hot in return and belted me one right there on the street and then when I try to protest he gave me another one, and then when I got mad and tried to hit him, he hit me again, and each blow was a resounding slap that cleared my head for new comprehensions. We were both screaming very loudly at each other, and as much hurt as embarrassed, I took off up the street telling Ray nothing, just leaving. No, I told him, "I'm through," and he hit me again as if to say goodbye.

And I just went up the road, left everything behind with Ray, and wandered around monuments and deserted lots while a Mexican jerk kept an eye on me from a distance. I was hurt and confused, decided almost immediately when Ray didn't follow me to double back. He had still been standing in the same place and when I walked back slowly with my head lowered, it started all over again, and as soon as I said something out of place and unforgiving, he hit me again—pow! My hearing was beginning to ache and I ran across the road almost getting hit by cars, and Ray was after me, this time I was trying to get away from him. A woman on a doorstep nearby called her family out to watch as Ray and I shouted at each other across the road. I was trying to get away, tired, and wanted a proper place to cry and get over it. I threw a rock at him and started getting far out in my panic, he finally stopped coming at me and called to me to say that everything was going to be O.K., I should just come with him and calm down, he started to walk west toward Mexcity along the road but kept turning back, apparently calm and wanting me with him again (I didn't love him any less) but I was scared and my pride was unable to take further falls and admissions of permanent despair that such fights could exist between us. I cowered in doorways of warehouses only waiting for him to go away and finally went with him to avoid the further scene of people watching, nowhere to go by myself, except to hell. We finally walked side by side, neither forgiving, neither speaking, past the police checking point for trucks which we knew was there beforehand—that's why our ride didn't take us through Puebla, for he was stopped earlier and told he would have to pay a fine for carrying a woman in the truck, so we got down. The police looked at us curiously but we just looked ahead casually as if it were natural for two gringos to be walking along the road dirty and homeless as we were. And the police guard said Adios, and we ignored him. We came to a bridge where I finally tried to say something to Ray, asked him how much change he had. He said, "two silver pesos," and asked why, and I said never mind, just give them to me and go ahead to Mexcity alone and don't worry about me (I featured suicide again—the water in the river below looked cool. I wanted to buy razor blades). He gave me the pesos and I walked back to the beginning of the bridge and picked a grassy spot by the river and watched the bridge to see him disappear, which would have been the end of it. He started to go but hung around looking at the water, and came back to me finally half an hour later. I had hoped for him to go, it was better for both of us, and I was ready to die, but scared that once he left there would be nothing else but death. But he came back to me just as I had begun to cry, to get it out of me—cried to end the misery. But he came back to me, and pleaded with me to stop crying, he could not stand it, he needed me, and so I got myself together and we went to the bridge again. He had promised me reconciliation in Mexcity, that we were just tired and hungry now, and asked me why I wanted the pesos. I told him, and he got disgusted, offended, frightened, and threw the pesos in the water. (I had given them back to him as a sign we were together again; he always holds the money.) Our last two pesos he threw in the water, but I was glad and contrite and the swell of fate began to recede in me though there was little to take its place except a plan to hitchhike. It was hot, and there wasn't much hope, but a car came quickly and picked us up, nice car, visiting businessman, took a fancy to me dirty as I was, liked Ray, too, so after we got over the numbness that followed our passions we talked to him of ourselves, contriving together to keep a continuity to our lies, passed through country where they had an apple festival and make apple cider and trees overhung everywhere with no grass underneath, bare ground, and looked at Mexicans, the market, swarming with flies that dug the apples. This town was like an old-time amusement park in summer, the grass under the trees tromped nonexistent. Ray and I began to feel better already. The guy who picked us up was plying us with flatteries about our romantic life which made us feel pretty good and enabled Ray to have fun putting him on. We drove the slow winding roads which approached the slow upward climb behind volcano Ixtaccihuatl, we passed road constructions for a new approach to Mexcity which made the trip only half an hour instead of one and a half hours from Puebla. (Puebla monuments through the air, the domes of churches like mosques in the distance, the entrance to Puebla a slow rise of hill. The aqueduct fractures reason with its arches still in existence, still in use from ages before when Indians had foresighted necessity, and it even survived Cortez.)

And we began to get really comfortable, I thought to myself maybe things will be all right after all. Evening starts to come—no, it is a thunderstorm come on us and drops of rain fall from individual clouds that have chosen hills to rest on. Mexico is a basin within a circle of mountains which is punctuated by the two volcanoes on the eastern side. Between the volcanoes is the easiest, most level pass, a natural entrance from Veracruz, Cortez found it and named it, but superstitions prevent it from being used. Even within the basin the altitude is great though in contrast to surrounding mountains it is low, and the approaches from all sides to the mountains are tortuous and strange in their variety. We were taking a route through the valley of Rio Frio, which is a valley by virtue of surrounding heights but very high also itself.

Mexcity. Close to Christmas. We check into a hotel in a different section of town than before. Everything is designed to make life as palatable as it can be with so many bad things happening that can't be helped; the object is to stay high and out of it and still operate to keep the money coming in and us fed and Ray writing poems frantically. The hotel is one block from Avenida Juarez and El Palacio de Bellas Artes where I had seen Sequiros' paintings six months before. Avenida Juarez is the main drag of tourist Mexcity and our hotel's street is a direct downfall to Mexcity low life, milling no-goods of the streets—mostly men, pimps, and vagrant types. The hotel houses mostly indiscriminate old men, transient lodger-types that hang out in the lobby, and the hotel desk looks like the entrance to a Turkish bath. I have to go through a scene with myself every time I go in and out of the hotel for there are so many regulars watching with nothing to do that it is obvious they must dig every aspect of every scene presented to them. (I am especially paranoid when a couple of times I drive up to the door in taxicabs with my john, or get delivered in a private car.)

It had been four months since we escaped the police in Texas and I figured that was plenty of time for them to be well on our trail and to have pinpointed us in Mexcity. Ray was out of the hotel a lot, writing poems he says, and often didn't come back all night. He takes to hanging out in all-night restaurants to write 'cause I am usually sick in bed or wanting to fuck or have some relief from the worry and monotonousness of paranoia and disgust at the apparently-permanent occupation of fucking a bunch of guys I don't like or have any interest in to get money for us to continue this way. It has no rewards for me; I am alone, lonely, bugged, feeling more and more unloved, as if each trick I turn is a negative score on the happiness list. Ray often spends all day walking in the Alemeda, a big park that stretches for five blocks; it is a central promenade area for tourists and tourist seekers.

Mornings we usually go to breakfast across the corner, buy magazines of Cinegraphics which show pictures of some good-looking chicks, artistically photographed in bikinis in Acapulco, and living the good life. I'm not sure whether I envy them or feel a kinship with them, for by now I have built up a defense about hustling that operates unconsciously and pertains to just about everything. So we sit in the morning sunshine from the windows of the restaurant on the street, getting warm. It is winter, Mexcity is damp and chill with an atmosphere of ill health that doesn't abate from day to day. The cold gets to your bones and heart. I hate Mexcity, none of the hotels—at least none we've been in yet—has heat, and most them have solid thick walls of stucco that sop up the moisture and cold and insulate the rooms into nooks of changeless atmosphere. You can take a hot shower and get warm that way, but the moisture from the shower mixes with the air and makes cold sweat, and there is nothing to do but cower between the sheets which are also cold and clammy—so we welcome the morning sunshine through the windows that for once keep out the cold. The restaurant is comfortable and it is the only bearable time of day, try to make it good. Ray will eat breakfast with me most any time, and that is some assurance of company. I try to be cool and nice to Ray so that maybe it will be a good day. Times have changed, he has started going to P's house without me, that means I don't even get my regular meager ration of music, and when I insist that he take me the attitude of us going together as happy joyful rocknrollers doesn't hold together anymore, it is apparent to everyone that we are miserable, forlorn....

Ray claims that he suffers as much as I do, and where he doesn't suffer he can't help me. In respect to fucking for money, that is my own gig and my own problem. I had some vision of writing being fun, a pleasure, a game that he was indulging in behind my back while I had to go out and get drunk and sick and fucked, and come back to loneliness, or quarrels. Oh shit, let me try to dig up a little joy here to interject—and in real life there was once and often joy here and there, simple stolen joy, get high on pot, and go out and eat in a restaurant and laugh at funny people. Look at the movie magazines and dig the chicks, I look out the morning restaurant window and feel the good sun, though weak and anemic, and I dig cats on the street. My vanity overwhelms me and I get a kick out of people turning around to look at me, bleached blonde, very blonde and I always wear shades.

I turn weak with hardship, dread, and worry. Trips to J's house, I am visiting there regularly. I have told everyone of our magnificent trip away from it all, though I give no details. Every time I go to J's house I come home vomiting, once with one man he made me take a drink that I didn't want and I, to my own surprise, ran to the bathroom and vomited it up on the spot; but that is later, an indication that I was pregnant and would have to decide to get an abortion, which was quickly done and over with. I convalesce one day and am back to flicking the next, no stopping in this game or you go under, and there's always the hotel to be paid.

So with that to face, my mind in a whirl, what solution to all of this unpleasantness, dig the map book with Ray, just come back and ready to go again already. The first night back into Mexcity chill, and unhealthy I say to myself let me out of here, immediately, this is death drawing blood out of the veins, Christmas Nirvana, the USA is preoccupied with its toys and sugarplums, even Mexcity gets into that spirit, tourists come and get a big bang out of spending Christmas on vacation in Mexico, shit. . . .

I still called Humberto O every time we were in town, and he would arrange to come promptly, promising to give me as much money as he could. I usually called him as soon as we got back into town so that we would have money to eat and smoke until something better turned up; he would go through the same cycle of fucking every time, go down on me, then me going down on him a little until I was almost to the point of retching, though I liked him and didn't want to show it, and then we would fuck, his little cock surprisingly straight and hard for such a little thing—and he knew how to ply it all right, so in spite of his overhanging baggage of stomach and old-age, flabby ass we made it O.K. He even got the idea that he could fuck me in the ass if he continued to try to talk me into it, so he would get to talking about that, but I put him down for it, only one guy got it into my ass and I was so drunk that time I almost didn't know the difference. Later with my pimp O I got so I dug it, pretending that I was getting back at Ray for his homosexual jail experiences, me so hip. . . .

O had been promising to introduce me to his brother who was a successful and rich businessman and government official on the side. O put him down for being more successful than himself and didn't associate with him much, figuring that his own life of easy going, in spite of the fact that he didn't have enough money, was better than all of that mind and life strain. O remained faithful to the revolution, and I think that's why I dug him, never got tired of listening to his stories though it got to be a drag having to fuck him for so little money. Sometimes he only gave me fifty pesos and bought me a cheap sandwich afterwards, but with him I tried not to be such a snob, and it was well that I did for he had turned me on to my initial sources of money which developed into a whole gamut of fucks. I was picking up information here and there from each new person I met that was of any worth. O had turned me on to Pilar the whore, who had introduced me to Emanuel de la G who had given me a list of whorehouses including J and so on till it built up to an impressive telephone book of scraps of paper I used regularly.

O finally talked to his brother on the phone, saying he had to call him about some business matter they both mutually were involved in anyway. He had told me that his brother fooled around a lot, never paid less than 500 pesos, and that if I played my cards right and went along with O's story that I was a student of his, hung up for money to get back to the States and not come on to him at all hip, act dumb, that I would be able to get him for a lot of money. Which O would be very glad to see, because he felt the money his brother hoarded belonged in part to him. I liked O; he called a cunt a cunt, called me a whore to my face, talked so casually that I felt less self-conscious about sometimes having to play the high-flown prostitute, and I have always put down ever playing an act as my sister always does. I don't dig false pride, I would rather show up to get laid dressed shabbily and cheap and as naturally pretty as I can, than be polished and expect that I am going to get around everybody by a bunch of lies. I much prefer to lay it on the line: look, I got something to sell and if you want it and pay me right, we get along, and I am not obligated to act otherwise, but O insisted that I had to play the hard luck student with his brother, and make like he was initiating my downfall....

I am always nervous making one of these telephone calls to a complete stranger to arrange for a meeting, figuring I am going to come on too strong and mess everything up or somehow get put down over the phone in some way that will hurt me, or even worse be given the runaround and somehow burned—the worst of all, that fear. But O's brother asked me to meet him at his office. He was busy for a couple of days and couldn't meet me right away but he responds to my come-on, I don't say much, O already laid I-don't-know-what story on him. I thought maybe O just gave me a runaround story and dually had given his brother the real story that I was a down and out regular, but I played it quiet and didn't say much at all, got dressed early in the morning a couple of days later, around eleven o'clock, and made it to the office building in the central business district two blocks from the hotel in the building where Sanborns had its big patio restaurant. (Sanborns is a chain of eating places like Howard Johnson where Americans go to get their breakfasts and are guaranteed sanitary holiday dinners, actually owned by Walgreen's drug stores, and a big hustling place obviously under the surface. Lots of Mexican businessmen go there to look and feel as though they are making an American scene, and lots of in-between hustling types go there to dig the tourists and Mexican businessmen-types, but do not often make a score there; it is too sanitary.) Up five floors in that building, the offices arranged around a central patio, into his office off a hallway around the corner. The lights are on in the office, good, he is there, everything is going smoothly, O.K. His secretary is a spinstress type who sizes me up with a look, so I speak in English to her (of course I speak no Spanish, dumb student type that I am) condescendingly and she shivers her disgust seeing through my farce right away. I sit in the office and neglect to pull my skirt down for her benefit for I figure that she is frigid to a point bordering on lesbianism, and maybe she will get a kick out of it. She takes my name and not-too-quickly admits me to the office beyond us both, as if I had an appointment at the dentist's. These office waiting scenes really give me the creeps. Soon O's brother comes out and shakes my hand and draws me by it into his office, his hand already lecherous in mine, I can feel it, and I sit on a leather chair next to his desk and he looks at me in silence with melting eyes. He is bigger than O; he has that big capitalistic grossness, and probably for the same reason, or other sets of comparative personality compensations, digs my thinness to the point of emaciation; I have gone hungry a lot. I get a kick out of watching his lecherousness in the presence of an avowed innocent student (did O have me pegged just right? I never all the time I was hustling did get over my attitude of amateurishness about hustling, every time I did it, it was because necessity forced me into it) and watching him get ready to come on. He contains himself pretty well in the office, only giving me one short kiss on the mouth, throwing in a kiss on the hand which I guess he thought was the quickest way to charm any young American lady, and I concentrate on just acting out further my natural fears and nervousness and come on shy and drop my eyes in a flutter of lashes that I figure a young American lady would resort to in a like situation, making what is disgustingly contrived a real true innocence, and I guess I did it O.K. He gave me the address of an apartment he said he and some of his friends use for parties; my heart leaps, is this an opportunity to occupy a pad? Can I twist this guy into a really good scene?

So I went to his pad that afternoon by appointment, and we sat in a room that looked like it really might be the main room of a clubhouse, chairs and a couch arranged in a circle in one corner of the room, a bar in an opposite corner with stools, and a great record player I get played tangos on. The porter is a pimp type. O's brother and I sit, I am dressed in some wildness of tight skirt and blouse that looks brazen without quite giving the show away and tell him lies about experiences I have had that I never really had but thought he would be interested in anyway. The conversation gets around to painting and I start expounding my love for Sequeiros, whom he is educated and hip enough to know all about, and he puts him down for being a revolutionary and a bad influence and says it is a good thing that he is in jail. Summing up his disapproval, he compares Sequeiros' irresponsibilities with his brother O and I hope I don't give myself away too fast, trying to keep control I stop talking just in time, before he is able to see that his philosophies disgust me. . . .

The concierge comes into the room from the kitchen where he hangs out, and at the master's request goes to a nearby restaurant to bring us menus so we can order some food.

Because we are drinking brandy, I am already over the initial buzz, and it is getting heavy, but he keeps filling my glass up and chiding me when it is empty. The menus come and he asks what I want—the opulent menu—I couldn't find a thing I thought suitable to eat;

everything promised to be very rich. The menu itself made me sick with its hopped-up interpretations from Spanish to English and he insists on reading over everything with me on the English side and I on the sly dig the Spanish but don't give myself away. Picking up on every opportunity to act dumb again, I express my cravings for simple meat dishes. There is nothing like steak on this menu, it is all gourmet concoctions and the only simple thing on it is roast goat, which suits him, too, but then he has to get involved ordering the first and second courses and dessert and this and that which starts getting interesting to me for I am hungry with all the brandy. When the order is sent off he starts getting horny with me, talking and kissing and running his hands up my legs under my skirt and managing to succeed every time in putting me in an uncomfortable position, sitting while he is mooching all over me. The addition of his breath to the brandy I have already drunk is overwhelming; I have already been there two hours and all this dinner business promises to last the afternoon out.

And I was right, it took us two hours to drink and eat dinner. He kept doting on me and the dishes, and I was forced to eat all of everything, though I resisted just short of the point of insanity. Getting through that dinner got to be a real bug, especially after the main course, but he dived in and with gusto praised everything. I decided to come on to him and get it over with as soon as I decently could. The kitchen boy settled the check, brought us coffee, and checked out for the afternoon, giving me knowing appraisals which he wouldn't do if he could dig that I was hip to it; there was a relation between him and the master which didn't include me, and I was obviously the mark in the crowd. I felt it, too, stuffed way beyond my capacity, uncomfortable, painfully bored, disgusted that such excesses of pleasure should go to waste on such a creep, but I tried to control my thinking and dig him for the future's sake. . . .

Sitting on his lap, reluctantly, I simulate great vapors of sensuality, moonings of affection brought on by his kiss, unbearable tantalizations of flesh I pretend throw me out of control. I go loose near him and make myself available, digging that his response to my act is wholehearted.

We move into a bedroom which has silk, flowered sheets on the bed and breezy curtains at the window. There could be snipers on the roof of the opposite building, there could be anything in this weird afternoon, it is all so beyond the reality I can embrace. He becomes fatherly and solicitous on entering the room, helps me remove my clothes, doesn't register surprise at my scanty bikini-type drawers which I always wear to accent the bikini suntan I now have. I brazenly plop myself right in the middle of the bed with them on, knowing that he would prefer me naked, but these cats just have to indulge my extravagances, and I am so full of food and drink it occurs to me that I could go to sleep very comfortably on these cool silk sheets. He has very carefully turned down the covers of the satin bedspread, removed his own white B.V.D.'s with his back turned to me and when he turns around I dig that he has the same small cock in comparison to his imposing stomach as O—a full life of indulgence told in his posture. I dig through closed eyes and don't hurry to move as he tries to get into the bed, lying directly side by side with me. But he changed his mind, got up, went around to the other side of the bed and let me lie there. I decided to give in to the stonedness, fuck him, let him service me at my pleasure, and he does actually go down on me with all of that food in his stomach and I figure if he is so disgusting, I am not going to have any compunctions, and don't struggle and dig it coolly until I get to a point where I can act like I am just waking up from a dream and make a few graphic movements that indicate where I am at. Every time I make one of these brazen movements trying to rush things he is caught between being surprised and digging it for the lascivious nature it expresses. He is all admiration (like looking at the menu, objective) of my looks, and I figure it is not impossible that it should really be so with my suntan so impressive in contrast to the yellow sheets. So I start taking control of the situation in preference to his keeping up with the fatherly bit.

I pull him up to me and try to get him to do it immediately, and he keeps me away momentarily but then gives in, making me first suck his cock for just a couple of minutes till it gets good and hard, small though it is, and we fuck side by side facing each other (difficult with all of his stomach). He tries to shift me around to different side positions to make it good, but finally turns me around and puts it in from the back which places the bulk of his stomach in a curve that can handle it and I am glad not to have to kiss him anymore and force myself to let go quickly, digging that this is not going to be any treat of surging masculinity. I jump around and twist my legs, holding on till I can feel he is ready to come and then seem to let go and do manage a little orgasm, the brandy interfering all along and going to my head, making it all premeditated in the haze of my mind, he comes, gasping delights of pain. I can actually feel his cock jerking stiff in me in sidewise moves too small for such a stiff peter; and then I immediately pretend that it didn't have anything to do with me at all, that I was asleep the whole time. He gets up and chides me for my laziness, goes to take a shower in the fancy bathroom where his clothes are hung, and I watch the breeze blowing the curtains, glad to have earned five hundred pesos.

・・・・・

One trip to J's house, an appointment kept—the cat was already drunk when I got there. He kissed me and I was somehow greatly repelled, he forced me to take a drink of brandy I didn't want and I thought it was just because I didn't want to make the scene, I could understand that all right, but what was this revulsion, my stomach gave me a queer jerk, the drink bolted, hit bottom too suddenly and I made it to the bathroom just in time, vomited something up and remained so dizzy and revolted-feeling that I could not stand up for ten minutes; one drink, that's all. J's pimp F knocked and came into the john when I didn't answer, the revulsion brought tears of frustration to my eyes, trying to get myself together so that I could face the cat again, worried, not needing the money any less than usual, he comforted me, asked me what was wrong. "What is the matter, Brenda?"

"I am sick, I cannot drink anymore, I don't know why, give me an Alka-Seltzer so that I can continue to put the show on the road."

He did, and I got myself together enough that I was able to service the john—he was so drunk he did not get too sidetracked by my strange behavior—the only quirk in the fuck was that I refused to do any more than let him crawl over me and have the play of the field all to himself, only passively participating, and he was disappointed that I wouldn't suck his cock. When I got home later to the Hotel C, cold wind blowing directly straight on through our door onto the balcony,

I staggered to the room out of the elevator, just barely controlling myself enough to pull myself to the room, my refuge. I told Ray about it and he didn't get as involved in my worry as I was, but put me to bed after suggesting that we should go out together (because I obviously couldn't?). He saw me to bed where my inertia took over, alcohol still bugging my system, and he went out alone. . . .

The next time I showed up at J's she started questioning me and asked me if I were pregnant. It did not occur to me that she was protecting a business investment, nor would it have made a difference to me whether she was thinking of me or herself, I was that close to her. (Though I did not ever trust J, always being very careful about being paid, and refusing most of her attempts to walk over me as if I were a possession of the house.) The doubt which was planted in my mind grew to a certainty through this talk. The next step in the interview was for her to lay the name of a doctor on me (I raised some objections—that I would just go for a checkup). I made an appointment with him for two days later. Ray wanted to consider it before I went, but I said it would do no harm for me to find out, I had already made up my mind; I didn't want anything growing in me that might threaten to bring another beauty such as Rachel into a sordid no-hope scene of life such as this we were going through. If I were pregnant it had to go immediately. I went soon to see the doctor, in his office (that was clean enough, but had too many magazines of a sort that did not reassure me, and chicks entering his office almost in tears). The chick before me was an Indian woman, market-type, poor, with two other children who were with her. I considered her problems, thought that maybe she had come for just a regular doctor's appointment, maybe she was getting care for the baby she was going to have, maybe I was the only person of my sort that came to this doctor for a while; but he talked to the chick of operations and reassured her husband who showed up after she had waited for two hours for her appointment, talked to them from his desk in another room. She is set for tomorrow. I found him sympathetic, but puzzling, for he didn't even examine me, just asked for symptoms and set me up with a time to see him the next day, asked me a little about J and talked about his office and got casual in a way that meant that he recognized me for what I was and had no objection or particular curiosity. He was just acting normal towards another whore who might have particulars in her background that interested him. Since I was an American he talked of New York, but the curious thing was that though we established this communication and mutual trust, there was no discussion of what he thought about my condition.

I went the next morning. Ray insisted on coming with me to help me through an ordeal that I did not consider as risky as he seemed to. He accompanied me as though it were his place; we waited nearby in a coffee shop for the doctor, late for his appointment with me. We waited nervously two hours and Ray said that he would stay downstairs in the cafe while I went up again (supposedly to be examined) and the doctor put me on the table, checked my stomach with his hands and gave me a nod, which was less an affirmation than a solicitation, and a shot of morphine. I woke through horrifying dreams later, through memories of retching and trying not to. I cried, pleaded the nurse to tell me it was done. Yes, she said, and pulled ten yards of bloody gauze out of my cramping womb. Ray came and immediately after I was conscious again and talking, the doctor came out of an adjoining room like a shifty old man. (I had been afraid to trust myself in a doctor's hands, especially one that knew my business. I thought I would get fucked over, and sure enough he had that look on his face, just as he had put me on the table before the operation. He hadn't consulted me at all, just said he was going to give me a needle, stuck it in my arm, and a warm glow came over me immediately. I smiled up into his face as I fell off backwards into sleep. It was my first shot of morphine). He asked me how I felt and led me into another room to show me the results of his examination. He started being very erudite, and held a section of vertebrate up in front of my face to indicate to me by size that the baby was two months developed. And I think I almost went crazy, felt everything of sanity slipping away and shouted to him to take it away from me, and cried, forgot about the nausea and vomiting and pain in my stomach. Let me out of here, no, don't you dare comfort me! Ray is waiting outside the office and protects me from the doctor and pays the money (I insisted that we not burn him though Ray hadn't wanted to pay the whole fee), took me home to the hotel where I had something to eat, and nothing was changed except I felt relieved of a problem. When friends come around to visit I was inclined to talk too much of my achievement, but Ray taught me to forget about it.

I had gone to J's the day before, and X Del Z was there, wanting me again; he was one of the men in Mexcity who never stopped wanting me. He was young, handled an important account for an ad agency near Sanborns' Reforma. This time he gave me his card and asked me to call him when I felt like it. We talked over my pregnancy and I came on as if it were his responsibility to help me—and he agreed to pay the five hundred pesos for the abortion. He was sad for me: some of the people that I knew in Mexcity I was almost completely open with, and laid all the details of our life on them. I didn't even want to fuck, pregnant as I was, and he had to talk me into it, comforting me to a point where I could feel grateful to him and feel a closeness on the bed. He suggested that maybe I just preferred to give him a blow job (his view of me as an anarchist chick reflects on me and I understand it too well, it was easy to know that he would pay for the abortion). I blow him with just the proper amount of subservience, and then climb over his limbs and get fucked just the same, no reason not to, but there is a great air of sadness all around me, and I am just going through the mechanics of being alive.

. . . Pachita came on to me with an offer about a rich man she could set me up with, and her attitude so clearly was businesslike that I knew instinctively she would get a good cut out of it. I thought I was always taking a risk of being cut short on my pay by these chicks who arranged things, but it turned out to be seldom true (that I know of) and I was sent to an address from her house, in fact she took me there in person in a cab, worried that I would not make the appointment. In the black night I get the nice feeling that it is a cloak and dagger romantic tryst in the night, her delivering me as the goods this way. And it was in fact weird, Pacha split out as soon as the introductions were made, told me to be a good girl (had told me to profess that I was a model), and the scene was an easy one for me, except for the quantity of drink. I walked into this little room where a table and surrounding seat like a cafe stall takes up one room that is filled with pictures of showgirls and clouds of incense that immediately make me say uh-oh, the atmosphere is so weird, and the cat himself is crazy in appearance, a stately faggot-type, his wristwatch prominent, his personal adornments—handkerchief and cigarette lighter—so gingerly a part of the whole come-on, and he likes to kiss and sit there with his dong hanging out his fly and once and a while apologizes to me for feeling my leg or timidly but insistently making me do this or that. The idea is to culminate in a blow-job. I get the idea immediately, and know that he is crazy, he is talking of all his successes—the excess of brandy causes me to feign interest—and I did wonder if it were all true. He pointed to the girls in the pictures as if they were his pet animals he brought into the world of fame. I wondered what he wanted with me, and consequently, to keep my head above water, stopped acting timid and acted as if I were something special too, not wanting to drive my deference to a point where I felt inferior. It was just a grope scene, he didn't come, I expected to fuck him but he kept it all in his pants somehow sitting at that table as if we were making lewd glyphs under restaurant conditions. He professed love for my young American good looks, but though he fawned over me I knew it was all a lie. I was just looking for an end to the scene, and it ended without climax and I was paid 500 pesos but got no fuck. He said that I was too young and beautiful to get messed up that way.

. . . Morning becomes more comfortable in Mexcity, knowing we are about to make another escape, Salina Cruz bound. And it's good to have money and eat and know that more money will be coming soon, and not worry about it so much, just let it come, the way it's supposed to, easy.

We had saved up just about enough money to go away to Salina Cruz, and thought it would be a really great trip because we had everything planned so well, and the radio to take with us, ought to be a lot of fun, and we had copped some pot, too, but figured we should have some security for the return to the city. We both were concerned of course about the bad scenes we ran into on the last return trip from Coatzacoalcos, and I for one wanted never to repeat them, so I decided to turn one more trick before we went, which money we would save to use for hotel bills when we got back to Mexcity, and that would make it all more charming and not so frantic and out on a limb. And how can you beat such a surely made plan as that—we really wanted this trip to Salina Cruz to be a ball. Mystically we knew that Salina Cruz was the place, and in fact it was an insight into some of the most important things in life, though they were all brought up out of the self like the sun coming up over my shoulder and illuminating the sea from a whole different direction, complete twist around all former traditions, the Pacific coast, and something in the name, too (Veracruz, or "true cross," as opposed to Salina Cruz, or "salt cross;" what are the connotations?). I get indiscriminate to the point where I am not able to figure how love can exist in all of this turmoil of not considering any one person more worthy than another than by how much money he has or how easy it is to get it; and even that flies to the wind, meaningless, when I get fucked, dig the person, service him, get next to him, do the bit, and then get burned. That's one of the main ways my head got twisted, for then it all became a lie. The climax came when Ray himself started digging people and saying that it had something to do with poetry. In other words he was doing the same thing as I was but on an intellectual, emotional plane that was, in his description, more interesting, more valid, than the straight hustle I had learned. He would get involved going to universities and digging students and I put them down as dumb, unworthy, probably because they were inexperienced; but Ray dug them, gets curious, and bugs me with questions regarding his untested homosexuality—

which I start to think has something to do with why we aren't fucking anymore. I really get bugged about it all, and there does not seem to be much in common between us anymore.

You who know me, I am beyond myself now, high and about to say goodbye to all of it, not just Mexcity and moods I cannot keep the idealization of anymore, and not just a sweeping trip to Salina Cruz. I didn't ever really lose faith in our ability to live together, but there was this personal sense that has to be satisfied. My mind is collecting up bits of defense to add to the block that is somehow half-consciously growing, that will make it all easy when the time comes to turn off emotion and say, well here is what I am going to do. I have seen enough hurts and mistakes to know that it doesn't matter.

When we got back from Salina Cruz and settled at the Hotel T we got a letter from the States—miraculous receipt of a letter with money in it was our first reaction—then reading it, afraid to face it. A New York newspaper reporter had chronicled Ray as a beat (beatific) poet when we first married (I had always put him down 'cause I couldn't reconcile myself to his middleclass attitudes, but now remember that it all started with me just teasing, being my regular silly self, forgetting the import that my words have on his ear, and he gets hurt). Ray got a letter from him as we dwell in the Hotel T, saying that it was all a mistake, that the police weren't after us after all, and he is impressed with some trivial irony that doesn't matter much. And I am immediately out on a limb with my loss, my god, irony, Rachel gone, half of myself fucked to the winds and things stirred up in me that I never wanted to see the light of, and irony doesn't just make me giggle or have a mental illumination, those moderations of reaction so small for me now, something twisted a knife in my very soul, and I have to run, the damage has been done, let me out of here, let me get myself straight if it is possible, and if it isn't remember that I always love you, Ray. I told Ray to go back to the States, everything waited for him there (I believed the letter). Told him that was what I wanted and the best thing for him, not to worry about me; that I would join him there in a little while. So it was that letter that did us in, that was the sign and the focal point.

Book Four

Mexico City and Back to New York

Introductory poem to the final book,
by Ray Bremser,
Rahway Prison, 1964

Tlalpan story:

the eschewed derivative;
from which the emolument stood out at attention
alarmingly / Popocatepetl simmering, meanwhile /
the outlandish Oaxacani waddled ...

time was, these experimental Rockies
withstood vainglorious invasions of prehistorical
gila monsters, terrible tarantulas, leapin' lizards of
   every imaginable description, pterodactyls,
   voluptuous vultures, brazen various breeds of
   brontocephalic buzzards, all beckoning
   —not to mention the nemesis erosion,
   or collusion, or corruption, or conditions
   otherwise quite
   improbable and absolutely impossible
   to catalog ... unobtainable ...

still the magnificent indian walks the ridiculous
   donkey path
   to the top
   where his incredible
   adobe-like-mudoaks-hut is;
   and the old lady, fat

   about to foal another piglet-niño they,
   for want of a better, shall call child,
   making the family
   seven adults and thirteen preposterous infants,
   four dogs and a burro, one rooster,
   one (similarly productive) peyotl-bush
and a still . . .

for example, like later,
the eschewed
   derivative
   (necessarily) derived and was wont
   to be called the eldest son of
   Juan,
      heir to a cave and one half an
acre of marijuana, mid the corn rows;
providing, of course, he survives
the disease presently leveling all and the rest of the
simple and
damnable family . . .

eschewed,
obscene,
indecent and live with the dry-rot
lewd as the whores of Acapulco . . .
infectious and done daily;
sold as
beautiful . . .

· · · · ·

So I am inclined to jump into things as usual; friends, you who know me, accept as innocent my stories, and ignore the fact that I do (just like all of us all the time in our hearts if we look) know what is happening.

Even my hustling got more blatant; my confession is not done and the point not proven. Life always sends quirks that make it right and necessary to renew anyway—even if the foundation is rotten—how we live this life, opium-smoked, illusioned, inclined to accept our own images of ourselves as having, oh I hope, sometimes come true.

So, to start at the beginning, we were staying at the Hotel T. It did indeed have regulated heat and it was a gas; it turned us on to comfort. We were really free agents and I didn't expect to get sick again. This was a pretty long stay there, about a month's time, and action-filled: out to eat breakfast we usually went to Sanborns, which is a group of American-catering lunch counters super-American drugstores, where they won't even sell Benzedrine, having picked up the American prejudice against junkies. We walk sunshine mornings under the Monument to the Revolution, over towards Avenida Reforma, the Reforma Hotel, Sanborns' restaurant where we eat biscuits with jelly or hot cakes and good coffee; they have these restaurants at strategic points all around Mexcity and you get a regular clientele that goes there and some hustle the magazine rack, and some just pretend to be doing their drugstore shopping. It is sickeningly Mexican-American, touristy, but we make it there regularly, as if it were our second home.

"Did Ray ever meet any of my Mexcity johns?" Now let me go through the list to answer that one. Sometimes Ray would tell me after he left me in a restaurant alone, hours later he would say he had left because he thought he saw someone digging me, and why didn't I pick up on that guy over there who was digging me? Anyway Ray starts getting down on me for passing up possibilities, and when I come back with no money from walking the streets we both came to the new idea that it was my fault, actively. And it could have been so, for I wasted time and money, and I fucked around with people, and I just walked the streets and felt like I only wanted to be left alone, and then people bugged me more, and I got mad....

Ray and I wondered what was happening in the world; we didn't seem to have any goal to achieve, and though we didn't come to blows over this experience it was one of the things that got us into such a bad mood with each other, as Ray figured that I didn't care for him, and would do completely independent things that I was actually opposed to—this incident was actually important in the build-up to my leaving him ... The day after I met up with Pedrito it was a sunny morning, and I woke up with the memory that he was to come to the hotel that day and I was looking forward to the three-way scene for a change. Sure enough, to my nervous apprehension, Ray and I had been having some kind of small falling-out (probably about money) just as he called on the telephone, and I didn't ask Ray if I should invite him over, but just went ahead and did it, presuming that Ray would be ready for any scene. He hadn't really said anything against it except that he didn't like Pedrito much, which I couldn't understand—but

I was sure that closer observation would change that opinion, so I told Pedrito to come to the hotel. I felt funny asking him, giving no particular explanation for why I wanted his company, except that we had agreed the night before to continue our friendship the next day. So Ray and I continued our discussion after I hung up the phone and, as I knew that Pedrito was due to show up at one o'clock, I was a little apprehensive since we were already arguing about nothing and I thought maybe it wouldn't turn out. My fears were proven correct when about 12:30, Ray walked out of the room angrily, with no word about when he would be back. I kept expecting him to come back, but it was Pedrito who arrived at the door, and I wasn't ready. I had been smoking pot, trying to figure things out, I guess, and he came in and didn't seem surprised that Ray wasn't there. I didn't have much to say to him, couldn't think of any reason for him to be there with me alone in the room sitting on the edge of the bed, but then I felt obligated because of our friendship the evening before, and we talked a little of that, because I was curious why he had acted toward me the way he did; yet I felt cold and distant, even with the pot, there was no reason to have this person here, no money was involved, and no love....

I kept waiting for Ray to arrive so that we could proceed, hoping that Pedrito would leave of his own accord. I rolled a joint, in my independent way, trying to show him hospitality, and sat over it with him with my head bowed in thought while he smoked, not knowing what to say, and he asked permission to kiss me. I didn't say anything, and he turned my head with his hand and kissed me but I didn't feel anything, didn't respond, didn't even recognize what had happened really, and just sat there, not saying anything. I was kind of stunned at the way things were going, and saw no reason to care or protest, so he pushed me gently back on the bed and took my clothes off, and I said something, yes, I said, "I would rather wait until my husband comes back before we do this." He didn't pay much attention to that except to move faster, I guess, and got my clothes off and studied my body a little and spread my legs on the side of the bed and went down on my cunt, his head between my legs. I had no reason to resist, and no reason to respond either, for I was looking at the ceiling and feeling the blank that had been made in my head when Ray left the room, and the bleak sunny Mexcity afternoon outside that didn't even penetrate to this inside room, though I knew it was there and irremediable. I've never felt like that before or since; had no sensation of importance, and no feeling of pleasure. I kind of watched him working on me down below but I didn't even feel any sympathy except that he was a guest in our room, and I let him take what was there to be offered. I kind of thought that my apathy would turn him off and he would stop, as nobody is so desirable that they can be completely passively enjoyed. There at least has to be a struggle of resistance to foster sensual pleasure, but he seemed to be content, and I was surprised that after he licked around for a long time, trying to arouse me, or satisfying himself, he got up on me, and I turned my head to the side and he fucked me. I didn't move and didn't feel anything at all and it was weird; he had taken his pants off but left his shirt and probably his shoes on, and he fucked me until he came. I didn't feel anything still, and I didn't come at all and the room was silent when he had finished and he retired to some inner portion of the bed and looked up at the ceiling. I got myself together and looked at him, got up on my knees and looked down at his face and felt sorry for him a little that I was such a bad hostess, and looked at his face which proceeded to seek my lap and looked up at my face, and I saw that he was a person and realized that I had just been fucked by him, and felt sad that I had given nothing and took his head in my hands and one of us cried, I don't know which, and neither cared to make an explanation; what point was there in my giving into humanity after the fucking was done? I just didn't understand at all. He said that he had been in a hurry to fuck me because he thought that Ray was coming back and that he was sorry, and I couldn't do more than look in the distance beyond the walls surrounding us and say, to repeat myself, that we were supposed to do it in Ray's presence. He got up and put his pants on, asked me to meet him at Sanborns that night if I could. Oh, I should record that before we fucked, or during the action I got a telephone call from one of my customers and talked extra brazenly and gaily to him over the phone, trying to scare Pedrito off, I guess, and he asked who that was. I told him and he acted surprised to know that I was hustling, and I put him down at that point saying that he should have dug it with Charlie the American tourist the night before....

Ray came back an hour or so later, no, just after Pedrito left, and the first thing he asked when he got in the door was had I fucked him, and I told him. He didn't ask for any explanations but went through a scene with me that he was going to leave me or something, and we fought and he threatened to hit me (this was my terror in those days: this violence got so overwhelming) and we came to a complete understanding. I never got a chance to tell Ray how it happened, except I said that I didn't want it to happen and that I blamed him for it because he left the way he had.

I grew to need Pedrito's comfort and his admiration, and his smooth looks. We spent the afternoon one day soon after I met him walking around on the streets, walking very slowly, as I was used to doing by myself, and he talked of his family in Managua, Nicaragua and how much money they had. We sat in a park not too far from the Hotel, too near in fact for comfort, but I didn't care. I felt self-conscious, for every time I got dressed to go out it was like I assembled a set of devices around me that didn't have any value or beauty by themselves, but just somehow held together and looked O.K. by the force of my need for them to do so. I felt very shy and like a young girl; he told me that he wanted to take me to Nicaragua where I would live like a queen and that was the life meant for me, because I was so beautiful. He told me that he couldn't see how I had stayed with Ray so long when I received the treatment that I did, and he didn't understand when I told him that I loved Ray, so I resorted to excuses about his being a poet and a beautiful soul, et cetera, to defend my love which Pedrito made me ashamed of. We sat in that park and somehow when he told me that bit about Nicaragua my soul soared, for I always knew too that I should live like a queen. But at the same precise moment that I was in such ecstasy my practicality, my perspective became reborn again and a silent voice inside me said, "he is lying," but I didn't care to listen to it, and besides I was too far gone by that time anyway.

But I didn't ever love Pedrito and I knew it. That is what is so hard to explain, and what was so confusing about the situation between Ray and me, too. You see, although I lied to Ray about the walks that Pedrito and I took together and the time that we went to J's whorehouse in the afternoon to fuck, that wasn't why I left Ray, and I didn't lie to him about the reasons I left him. I kept my affairs with Pedrito a secret, too, after I found out how much it hurt Ray, because I didn't want to hurt him, and make him think that I was leaving him for someone else. I just wanted to make it clear to him that I needed time to straighten out my head, for I couldn't cope with violence and arguments and images of ruined love. The key point in my leaving Ray, as much as finding a security of companionship in Mexcity, was this letter that we had from a newspaper reporter in New York City, whose inaccurate information we were mistaken to trust, that Ray had been cleared in New York. I thought that Ray would want to go back, and I wasn't ready to go, but I thought it would be good for him, so when I said goodbye to him I thought I was being kind.

Now I have no muse to resort to, no sun to proclaim, no babies to worship, no steadfast love to defend myself with, no roads and mountains to climb with my eyes seeing freely, nothing but my own heart to search out in cold Mexcity, and keep Pedrito close to me as an excuse for being so alone, and say "I love" to him, to keep him close to me and insist that he say the same to me so that I know that I will not be alone unless I want to be. So I send Ray away, I send him away; Ray, don't you think I can get along by myself, I have to prove something. These were the actual arguments I gave him, though I wandered the streets with Pedrito, and saw things I hoped never to experience, the loneliness of a street corner, the self-reliance of staying out all night because there is no place and nobody to go home to, and no expectation of it. I was alone in the world, and why not, why not?

But the Mexcity time-snake in my head still sent me into the streets in search for something; something besides money.

The day that I left Ray I patiently waited; I knew that he would go out. I told him that I wouldn't be there when he got back, gave him some idea that I would be out trying to score, and that I was determined to succeed, so that he might expect me to be gone a long time. After he left I got dressed as practically as I could, knowing that I would be in the same clothes until I was able to make things straight for myself. I wrote a little note, trying very hard to make it clear that we were through (I can't take it anymore, Ray) and telling him not to try to find me. Then I struggled with my still-existing love trying to incorporate into the note some feeling of kindness that would preserve him from hurt, and yet ruthless at the same time, having come this far, determined not to turn back or be thwarted. I had no consciousness of having done this before, though I had written just such a goodbye note to Ray when we were separated by jail just shortly after our marriage, and I had expressed my refusal to accept any more of life in the same situation—though I couldn't pose any alternative to it except escape. Then I did a cowardly thing which I thought would gain me some time before Ray was on the track after me—oh, no, I think I told Ray I was going to P's, telling him that I was sick of the situation and had to hear some music. Anyway, I left the note at P's house, not at the hotel; walked to P's house in the Indian dust and left the note there for Ray to find later when he started wondering what had happened to me. I feared my own action, but also the possible miscarriage of it.

Now I was free to think and fear for myself. Now I was free from one half of my problems, whether Pedrito wanted me or not, and I really didn't know about that. I didn't tell him any of my plan, though I hoped he would help me once it was done. I looked forward to getting some reward for my pains by having the freedom to gratify myself completely with Pedrito now that there would be no interference from Ray, if Ray would leave Mexcity and go back to New York (which was what I hoped). That letter we had received stuck in my mind, that Ray was now free in New York, so why shouldn't he return and live a life of no pain, as I intended to do? But I didn't see Pedrito at all that day, though I searched for him everywhere, my new freedom of moving sending me into long walks with no need for fear of hurt, for what did I have to be robbed or cheated of more than myself alone on the streets? Something was sure to show up that would take care of me. I had been involved in human nature too long not to have at least half a hope that any stranger on the street would help me if they could. All of the guilt of hustling went down the drain when I left Ray, for now there were no barriers of opinion or hurt but my own self and human nature for me to make my way with, and that's not scary really, except in the acknowledgment of cold and hunger when my plan didn't work, and this was something to think about. I had nothing to fall back on in Pedrito, for he didn't have money, nor a place where he could take me. He hadn't even wanted me to leave Ray, and even after I did, he tried to reconcile me a little to Ray so that I wouldn't have to wander the streets, and could at least go back to the Hotel and have a place to stay the night. But despite all this, I knew that it had to be faced, and the break made, and then, or I would never be able to do it.

But damn! It was cold those nights and days, though the days had some sunshine, and I had even become used to discomfort during the day since the beginning of our stay in Mexcity, when I had to hustle during the day. Then there was no choice; hustling or hunger and arrest were the possibilities. Then I got used to being uncomfortable all day and often late into the night, but this was even worse, this wandering all night with no place to stay, no security in the world, not even trusting my legs to keep me walking all night and hoping I might be able to make a streetcar ride take enough time so that maybe I would step down from the streetcar at the end of the ride with some idea of how to take care of things. I guess I spent a couple of weeks time homeless this way, with nothing protecting me from the world, hoping that Ray would get out of town quickly; maybe I was beginning to feel his paranoia of being hunted (is that what bugged him all the time in Mexico? . . . For I myself had a fear of police and a feeling of desperation, but I never felt alone, and I guess that Ray bore the brunt of the fugitive situation), so that I could feel safe and settle down. I could feel his presence, mourning, raging, and looking for me, as much out of pride as hurt and love, and I thought maybe he would kill me. What use was I to him now, I had made that clear, and if he succeeded in capturing me what complete desolation of humility would be done on me? Yes . . . I feared Ray greatly. . . .

This is a sad dance I do on the streets; I found Pedrito at Sanborns and walked miles of Mexcity cold, the stucco houses uninviting, all the world shut in as I walk the streets, say it, yes, without love. Why have I turned out so? And I spent one whole night after walking far, with Pedrito. We smoked some remainders of pot I had brought with me from the stash at the Hotel T and he got silly, and probably horny, scared to smoke on the streets till I showed him the easiness of it; it doesn't matter if people were around, it all goes up in smoke anyway, see? I tried to show him some other things, too, and put some very definite commitment on him for love, and he admitted it, and I felt the victor, now I could arrange things as I liked, having gotten him to say the words. . . .

It was a struggle of more or less equal wills with Pedrito and me;

we were both the same age—23, as I found out when I finally got a look at his passport. I had thought him so much older—I had accused him of being thirty years old, and he didn't answer yes or no till I found the actual truth from his passport. I had relied a little on his more mature experience till then, and then I found out that I had been overestimating my equipment; in fact, that held true with the whole experience. Pedrito didn't at all meet my expectations of having something true and strong to guide me, and I very quickly knew how much it was all up to me.

The first night, pitifully, we rode back and forth to Xochimilco on the longest streetcar ride in the city, oh praying for dawn to come soon for I was so cold. I never had proper clothes to wear in Mexcity, and the cold damp is often inescapable, especially in Xochimilco where all the bad airs from the whole Mexcity basin settle, for it is the lowest spot and swampy; we rode on that streetcar with all the world in misery and he slept with his straight black hair in my lap. I had to have pity on him as I did that first day in the hotel room there, maybe because he was as alone in the world as I was, though he claimed he could handle it. I guess he did get along all right, a sad and lonely existence and God! I really did feel sympathetic, if that is anything like love, and I told myself that it was at least enough, and admired his long black straight hair and knew that more than all the world I wanted to make some claim to Indian heritage.

I couldn't see into the future at all, for the future was an empty lack of vision, lack of ambition, lack of image, and only the trick to turn that night excited me, and the time that I would spend with Pedrito in making it possible, though it was more drug than anything, a preoccupation with brushing teeth and getting everything in good working order—"beautiful" Pedrito would say. He wanted to make me "beautiful" as he knew I could be. Though this offended me a little, I did become more smooth, in looks and hustle. I came to agree with him and we talked of clothes and he encouraged me in all artifacts of beauty I showed an interest in, the first being my dyed hair.

I heard something one time, some saying, that there is nothing more phony than a reluctant prostitute. Well, usually I felt that this was true, but one time it worked fine. . . .

The night's sleep was gone and the alcohol petered out, causing me to wake from sleep; this happened every day about one in the afternoon. Maybe it was the crowds across the way, all teenage Mexicans waiting to move into the theater about one o'clock; that's when we always woke. Always me first, wanting to get up but wanting to stay down next to unmistakable comfort, watching the gray hotel ceiling, the chick in the hall knocking on the door to clean the room, Pedrito shouting "mi amor" to the door, calling to the maid to come in and jive with him while we lay there, and she would come in and get turned on to whatever alcohol we had around while Pedrito taught her to say "fuck your mother," which he had picked up from me. This got to be a big thing with him—that this cleaning chick dug him, and he gave her all kinds of little gifts like the socks he replaced with new ones later, or shirts, or shoes. She, very businesslike, accepted everything and giggled, slouching further over her broom mop, saying, "fuck your mother," or telling Pedrito about men in the hotel who liked to look at me.

Showers would be next. Pedrito went first, out of consideration, because I liked to lie abed awake and smoke leisurely, listening to him singing; unreasonably, he would come back too soon for me, digging the white ceilings, towels wrapped around him, steam pouring out of the shower. A middle-aged wakeup Turkish treatment he gave himself, and I would never realize how serious it was for him, till I dug his concern with whether the toothpaste was running low or whether the towels were clean. I got up next and quickly dressed in whatever clothes were closest, while the maid lingered outside our door, waiting to be invited inside by her great friend Pedrito.

None of this contented me in any way, or ever did, except when something was bought for me. I walked down the sidewalks, and when I was alone everybody said small words of threat to me. I ignored them in contemptuous ways that indicated that Pedrito was the only Mexican I was interested in. I moved into the delicatessen to make my purchase, got the bottle open, and hurried upstairs to the room, planning an afternoon of creative drawing and painting, took my clothes off and sat opposite the mirror on a dresser top and tried to dig the beauty of my face that had everyone so mystified, or at least me. I wasn't able to see it exactly in the mirror, except in attitudes of laughter or exaggerated wings of eyebrows, striving, torturing my head with the inability to capture what was right there for me to see in the mirror. But I tried, and drank myself to sleep the whole afternoon, or gave up and read a book, evil de Sade, which made me hot for Pedrito to come back quickly to the room on a day that had become so quickly evening. He came in and dug it, and I got him to fuck me again before the night came. Then I had to assume my character, which was the final blow. So I dug fucking him and consumed it as neatly as the bottle of wine had gone, and when it's over realized the cold. Pedrito reminded me it was time to get dressed.

Feeling rebellious, I wore a tight black skirt, sandals, and borrowed his tan sweater with a big meshed t-shirt, which I pulled down tight into the skirt and felt very comfortable, because the sweater was so big I could hardly be mistaken for having any great consideration for others' tastes. I tied my hair up the back of my neck, getting it just right in the mirror, reflecting back the sweet images of red cheeks from heat rash which I exaggerated with paints, and dug that at least I could paint me, for real....

Ernesto Z, shiny part-Irish "Mayor" of Mexcity, thought he was Don Quixote still on the hoof, literate translator of the same: I met him one night at the Hotel Del X—where I was sitting alone drinking by myself, and this distinguished little man said, "would you like to join our table?" I looked over to the table where three men and a chick craned their heads around to look at me and smile. I immediately got scared and said no. The little man retreated, hurt, and I felt glad, and turned back to my beer, cheeks burning. Next came this big grandfatherly type and spoke to me very politely, courtly, and I went with him. Later he would teach me to dance the paso doble, but now I just tried to hustle him.

He introduced me to the people at the table, two men—and I thought of hustling all of them. The young distinguished one I had refused introduced himself as the Archduke. We sat and talked, I never remember what people say because I don't talk or listen, just sit and answer what's directed at me and dig the compliments I get, which that night was mostly from Ernesto who was ecstatic about my face. He was, in fact, ecstatic about everything he liked; when the music came on he raised up his arms and sang, raised up his neck and sang with it. I figured the first night with him that he was a silly old man, but I was too nervous with the possibility of making money to put him down. As we left the Hotel Del X—I was acting as though I had to go home, and Fedrico was trying to get me to come with his friends and him for some fun. As soon as we got to the staircase outside the hotel, I took the arm he offered me and told him in a small voice that I needed five hundred pesos. He was very surprised, and pleased, and said that I would have it.... I drank too much, ate steak, and danced good dances with him the place we went, a dance hall, a huge nightclub with a great complicated menu. He dug me across the table and I felt almost like falling under the table, it got to be such a thorough digging, he wanted to watch every mouthful go into my mouth, telling me later that he loved to see women eat meat... and I was the animal for him.

In the taxi which waited for us everywhere we went, he kissed me with a mouth so inquiring I almost got paranoid from the insistence of it.... I dug the dancing with the saxophones, especially when there was someone who could channel my sensuality into forms of sociability. Ernesto dug showing me off because it was to his own benefit. This was fun for me, after all the cats so hung up with just rubbing up—once they know they're going to have to pay for it. He looked pretty good himself, so tall and skinny with white hair and funny side teeth that stuck out from hollow jaws, and he always held his head and shoulders up in his perfect suits with such elegance himself that it made me feel good that he thought I was the most elegant he had ever seen. He called over a photographer girl who took a picture of me with my drunken eyes closed, which drew compliments of "madonna!" The band kept starting up again, but I didn't like to seem too athletic and actually was feeling sick, so I pleaded that we leave.

I was anxious to go somewhere and fuck him so the money would be secure, but I had already begged him that I had to be given the money ahead of time, and though he was puzzled, he gave it to me and I stashed it in my bosom. The sickness was impending and it was already late into the morning, and the Mexcity chill was almost too much for my sandals. We made it to the Turkish bath.

The veneer of elegance weighs on me. As Ernesto Z fucked me that rainy chill night, steams of vapor rose from the Turkish bath. The taxicab awaited us outside in the courtyard, where we had approached and blown our horn for the corrugated doors to rise. I cried as he fucked me; the removal of my underclothes was frantic and I cried; it could have been any night from then on that I got in the same condition of despair. E brought it all up to me clearly.

God, I wanted out of this. I had wanted out since Veracruz, but hadn't been able to see the way, and now it lay before me: the last escape, back to New York. Do you understand? Do I have to tell this story on into the night, telling away the sickness? How I went to Acapulco for my health and saw everyone getting fucked for money there, too? The whole world was sick!

What is all this lack of love? We who started with so much love; can it be depleted the same as health? Or the same as desire? It amazed us in its going; I found I did not love Pedrito, merely used him to escape Ray. And why had I wanted to escape Ray at the very time when joy should have begun to overwhelm me? . . . Because my faith in life had begun to fail.

In bed I cried, for when the climax came it was only a fountain of tears opening to me dangerous territories which might have been love, had I not been so twisted. E was experiencing love for the first time in so long, he didn't know what was happening, and couldn't prevent what I was able to do to him.

I took more interest in the bathroom douche than an intelligent whore should, and E took my interest in my store of Hoboken obscenities (I had told him I was from Hoboken, which to him was the center of American decadence and anarchist beauty) and loved to hear me expound on life in terms of fuck and cunt, cock and prick, and other variations he had never heard from a chick's lips before.

Ernesto Z often made diplomatic trips to Washington and told me of the beauties of the Pan American Union. Secretly he admired the States more than Mexico, but he was confused, because his mother was an American and his father Spanish-Mexican. So when he raised his arms in praise of a Mexican song it was as someone who knew what it was about, but he also had a strong idea of the traditions behind it. He insistently claimed that American women were the most beautiful in the world and the rest of the countries could go to hell for all he cared; though, being of a diplomatic turn, he knew ways to put a country down without getting too involved, and he would curb my impulses to talk of revolutionary activities, saying it was childish. Besides, being a landowner, he sincerely dreaded another revolution in Mexico, which would leave him without his dreams of self-sufficiency. I kept up my revolutionary talk whenever able, to bug him about this, and saw him cringe, square and bourgeois as any merchant, for all his nobility, scared that the next day's bread would not come easy. He knew that I was giving him a workout, but I protested anarchy, not communism, and he was welcome to his bigger portion than the rest, if he was able to hold on to it. He professed that he would like to hand it over to me, and have me, the queen of anarchy, minister to his needs.

So I was being influenced on two sides, and took both seriously: Pedrito, who was living the life with me, and Ernesto, actually doing the same, though it was different. In truth Ernesto was a better ball; experience does count, and Ernesto had escaped the threatening fag element by throwing himself so fully into degeneracy that it didn't do much good to suspect him of anything. When I was with Pedrito I fell back into a kind of torpor, a sick life too full of richness, whereas Ernesto, the rich one, ate melon and salads if he ate at all, and I had pure meat feasts to give him the pleasure of watching my teeth working. Pedrito began to get fat from so much eating all the time and sitting around doing nothing, not even worrying. I lied to both of them, forgetting the other when I was with one, and a voice in my head told me to go ahead and be savage with all men if I want. . . .

Then there was my affiliation with the lesbians at the S Cafe, where I had been dropping in since I left Ray; it was a refuge, and I liked to see the beautiful Mexican and Cuban lesbians. There was a short blonde chick there, with the same savage look around her teeth that I figure is a sign of depravity. She wore slacks and nice bright ponchos and played a guitar against her leg and sang in that deep-from-the-heart voice that is a gift of the Mexican chick; she would sing those ballads like her heart was broken, and it cracked me up, so I went to visit them with Pedrito. They would smoke my twists of pot, and Pedrito would dance with a straw hat until his teeth flashed, and I would think that I wanted to fuck right there with all the excitement. But I was shy, and the blonde chick would sit next to me, or stand behind me and look over my shoulder, her hand so soft, and hypnotize me with her eyes. I let her kiss me, wondering, and her lips were the softest-sweet kiss, but Pedrito flipped out with jealousy and we had to go.

It was a cold night and the rain was dripping outside. There was no hurdy gurdy to serenade my evening; I could not dig the pigeons or the sun setting reflected on the yellow wall of the movie theater opposite. All the world was compressed with the cold of the rain into our hotel room. Next to ours the Italians were singing the joy of nighttime dinner on the hot plate, and it was almost time for me to perform—I mean hustle.

Mexcity is called in all tourist folders the city of eternal springtime, but it is more well known by those who live there as a place of germ nurture. Flu germs once set loose into that air spread in hopelessness of complete takeover, and everybody gets sick and stays that way, except for the Indians, who have some built-in resistance that had become traditional by killing off the unfit. All other people, once they got sick, stayed that way until they went away to a more benign climate. Sure, the flowers bloomed and strawberries always made it down from the hills to market—but I craved the sun like a reptile.

The night air was cold as I made it out onto the street, dodging the rain, into the arcade of the Hotel Del P, past the downstairs Sanborns' restaurant and Pam Pam, which cracked me up with obscene fruits in the window. I went in there once and sure enough there wasn't anything good about that place, old lady tourists lunching on a lunch hour forced on them by the rigors of their tour schedule. They all gawked at me as I walked past, self-conscious that my legs looked "fine" and everything was so much in order with me that I felt ashamed for them because of their reaction. So I sauntered through that slippery floor area in the bottom floor there under the hotel cavalcade of restaurants, valets, and shops that sell gloves and lacy Mexican shirts and awful old-lady bathing suits that nothing but resort places ever have the nerve to display.

As I walked up the carpeted stairs to the lobby regions of the hotel, the doorman knew me, and was half polite and half familiar. I cooled him with a stare that said I was capable of anything, and continued my walk upwards past jive young men who thought it was free at cocktail time and almost confused me with their compliments, for my gig was real ladylike now and I just couldn't turn and say some vulgarity which would without a doubt have turned them off. As I reached the door of the Hotel Del Z, I paused, posing, letting my eyes get accustomed to the atmosphere and wondering who was there. The piano was already tinkling, and if the chick player whom I got to know there would be playing a good entrance tune for me all the better, for I dug it that way, and smiling at her in passing, made for a table by myself.

The dark air illuminated various sections of the leather room, which would have made a good setting for warm pictures, but instead they had watercolor tourist attractions—girls doing Mexican gypsy dances.

I allowed myself to be talked into sitting with two guys who posed themselves as friends of Adda, the piano player (she was a blonde Yucatanean who carried out the myth that all people from those parts are artists, and she really laid it on thick, imparting soul to popular songs by great weight of water-falling keys improvising concertos. I dug it, and the way she got dressed up in fantastic great dresses full of heavy material that showed her big blonde bosom and small hands. She often came on to me about my sad face, and I was touched that my situation aroused sympathy in her; I did sketches of her when I lost interest in hustling the clientele). So I figured they were cool, but it then took longer to get to the point because I feared the humiliation of getting kicked out of that place, and also had to be discreet on Ernesto's account.

After many drinks and almost unbearable come-ons about my appearance (something in Spanish like I was the greatest doll that ever hit the scene), when I made my pitch the guy came on as though he didn't think it would be right to do such a thing with me; but he did agree finally, though the situation was unpleasant, because he was trying to reach my legs under the table and directing smooches at me across the top. But all restraint dropped as soon as I laid my cards on the table. I suppose it was a mistake for me to do so with him, though he came on so big that I couldn't resist, and maintained the illusion in my head that something good would come of it, despite the horror of his behavior. He insisted on inviting Adda to the table for a drink, and I was relieved that she took it at the piano. It sat there untouched next to a vase of roses.

I couldn't understand the complete switch-around of this cat; his young Mexican looks were not too threatening, like a pampered son who had reached later youth and was still pampered; there are lots of them in Mexico. I thought the reality of the situation would override everything and I would just have to put up with the unpleasantness, so I drank with him for torturous long hours, and finally told him I was going to leave, for it was getting very late. As I went out into the night with him and walked under the lonely street lights of early morning, he treated me like a longtime girl friend he didn't have to be very polite to.

I was always afraid that I might run into a stray F.B.I. agent and be busted after attempting to hustle him. This cat in the middle of our drinking showed me his police credentials, but I laughed, figuring it just another Mexican bureaucracy quirk; all Mexicans work for the government and have honorary titles with imposing meanings and no work to do.

He showed me to his car and drove to the outskirts of town. I anticipated an eerie draped motel, but worse, he stopped in a deserted area of blackness and proposed that we neck, so I asked for the money first, and he said he was not going to pay and started to grab me. I could see his cock already out, and he was jerking off. I tried to get away, with one hand pulling my switchblade, and the click in the dark scared him so much I felt come in the tussle, and made it out the door frantically getting myself decent. I ran up the street where with luck I got a cab just as he started the pursuit behind me in the freeway night, the blind cars lonesome under fluorescent road lights. I recognized his car following and anticipated a bust all the way into town, nervously realizing that escape was impossible—and my heart fell as I saw he intended to follow and continue his sadistic pleasures.

. . . . .

I kept a picture of Ray, a little one that appeared in some stateside newspaper article about a poetry reading or parole arrest; I treasured it because it was funny and vulnerable looking, and Pedrito tolerated it for the same reasons. Though I was truly indignant and hurt towards Ray still, I made an even bigger show of it to Pedrito. I knew from Irving that Ray was already making the poetry-drug scene in New York, and it was unclear whether he was truly free of the law or not. I just got bugged at hearing anything about him at all, and even more bugged when I got a letter from Ray himself, speaking to me in very condescending tones and demanding that I send him some pot, and for me to follow it immediately or we were through forever; he said this was my last chance:

Dear Bonnie-

I am going to obey what is the form and laws of the heavens. Everything is happening so fast and precise, I can do nothing else. You have not got the right to hang me up with your indecision like you did before in Trenton. You must write an immediate and direct note or letter telling me you'll be back in three weeks, on April such-and-such; or five weeks, whatever the duration of your intended absence. Or, if we are through, you must tell me we will never make it again, and release me from my hung-up swearing, obligating me into the netherlands of eternity after my death. In making the action of leaving me, you have suspended (at least) and cancelled out your own!—I've written you four or five letters, but not sent them; I am heavily confused, and sniffing H and cocaine, not healthy hung elsewhere. Do me the favor. Love, Ray P.S. Send some goodly-wrapped pot firstclass airmail Jo K city desk New York Post, New York—it's cool! (If you ever need loot, ask me) R.

So, I have to reproduce one of the actual ones he never sent, though they were all alike, all four or five of them. The one I received in Mexcity I tore to pieces and threw immediately away, indignant, confused, and not wanting Gonzalo to interfere by reading or commenting, chastised Irving for giving Ray my address. Yet deep in my heart I was glad he had written me for all the offensiveness of the message, and I stored it away and wondered what would happen if I didn't get back in time. In reaction I sent Irving pictures I had drawn of Pedrito asleep nude on the bed, knowing that Irving would dig the shape of him. I had written to Irving earlier that I wanted the marriage certificate from Ray so I could get a divorce, and actually did get this from my father who was glad to go to the bureaucratic trouble for such a worthy cause, and followed soon after with the hundred dollar check, with a note to the telegraph office that it couldn't be cashed except by me personally, because he didn't trust the company I kept.

So life was all very confused, and I concentrated my mind on the goal of getting to Italy. My farfetched desires were the most clear-cut to aim for; everything more close was too confusing.

The night was smoothing over Mexcity, black smooth hair streaked with some Spanish wax. The night lulled over the obscene exposure of the day, and all flowed into a black dress—the Mexcity night of Indian hair where each strand has a meaning in life.

Ernesto Z was saying goodbye to me again, and for the last time. He kept telling me that money no longer allowed, and his heart was breaking that I was destined to be a whore. Once again we were making it out onto the scenes of the Mexcity night together; just one last fuck, Brenda, he said; he couldn't resist me.

We had talked of an Indian dancehall he wanted to take me to in order to show me what low life was like in Mexcity. He said when we went there I would see how Indians survived the overgrowing of their civilization. He looked down his nose at the Indians, but I raised my voice in praise, saying that one Indian footstep on those hills out there was worth more than all his Spanish-Mexican properties multiplied by years of tradition, but the struggle was no good, and I decided just to allow him to have his whim. I couldn't really expect a john to agree with my heart's beliefs anyway. (Jack M had told Ray and me of a dancehall on the outskirts of Mexcity where you could grope a chick in the gallery for a peso, cheaper than Veracruz or Mexcity marketplace whores, where the standard lay was five pesos.)

So we went, and that was about the third stop in our evening. We had drinks at the Hotel Del P, dinner at the Hotel H, and then made it to the Indian place, for Ernesto wanted me to learn to dance the Damon (deep Indian dance, belly of the snake slithering across the floor, Indian prostitutes in red shoes and ribbon-braided hair, snakes' head figures protruding from the corners of the ceilings with red lightbulbs leering out of the open fangs, the bar mahogany with plaster snakes coiled all around the edge in cornices, the music became a drum throb from underneath it all). We were treated with the deference of tourists but I was relieved to find Ernesto knew some of the musicians, and finally a waiter came to serve us cheap rum in the booth we had picked, where damp reptile airs crept up my skirt. Nobody took notice of my morals, they were more interested in my ass, so we danced, and Ernesto swerved me around the floor in all directions, so that everyone would get a chance. The other dancers left the platform digging that they were being given a show, and I blushed in excitement as the photographer's camera clicked.

And the flutes and the drum beat, and the saxophones groaned into the beat of the indignant Indian will, the danzón at the hardest hump, the back of the snake slowly heaving all Mexcity through its everyday convulsions of Coca-Cola, and only the Indian knew, all the Spanish denied the still great threat of final revolution in Mexico City, the Indian overthrow. But these taxicab drivers and Indian whores were too far gone in it to care about my ideas of religion. They were gone far out in the participation and the dance. Ernesto wanted to dance every dance and put me through some toils that night for my fee....

But the next night it was goodbye again, and a different scene; we went to a restaurant that had French cooking and Spanish violins which played the paso doble. I was initiated in the physical whirls of the ritual dance; the chick acted as a cape; all her step movements and flying out into the middle of the floor to simulate the twirlings of the cape, and the man of course was the matador, who always kept his partner working in steps backward to have her in better control. This is one of those dances everyone participates in unison in, even in that restaurant cocktail atmosphere, and the meaning of the dance is apparent by the figure the chicks make all whirled to the center of the floor at once and the men holding them at arm's length. The dance went on and on in a circle of repetitious double passes that never lost their excitement....

And then one afternoon it really was goodbye, for the next day Pedrito would take off for Nicaragua, and I was scheduled to leave for the States, soon as I had got my packing complete. I saw Ernesto one last time and he gave me a silver cigarette holder which was a feminine mate to his own which he had bought in a cigar store on 42nd Street. Yeah, coffee that day, and I wasn't sad to say goodbye, but felt bad that he was taking it so hard.... Yeah, I was ready to go....

And Pedrito? He bought fancy suitcases he insisted were such a good buy, so that he wouldn't look shabby while he was visiting with his family; he even tried to give the old ones away to the chick who cleaned out the hotel room, not even thinking about what I would use to cart my stuff to the States in. He gave me devoted promises that we would be reunited immediately, as he would only stay in Nicaragua for a couple of days. I devotedly vowed how much I would miss him just that short time, and didn't really care whether he showed up again or not, except that I would get burned out of the money I had given him for plane fare, and the extra so that he wouldn't have to greet his family with empty pockets. Yeah, he took off from the hotel one morning and I was alone in Mexcity for one day, actually alone, waiting for the next day to come, with nothing to interest me except my prospective departure, and the anticipation of pangs I would feel at leaving Mexico. I dug that however circumstances arranged themselves I was walking out of the darkness of death and secret life into the light of exposure, and I wasn't sure that I would dig it. I stayed in the hotel and awaited the next day with fear, the dawn to send me into flight from a year's occupation here back into a way of life I had forgotten the existence of. Whatever it was I was trying to express there in Mexcity had long since reached an anticlimax anyway, and I was dragged....

This perspective dawns on me as I leave Mexcity, into the cab as if I take off for a trip, but different, knowing that this time everything fades behind me maybe forever. But I didn't make it out of the country so easily. At the airport I had to get my baggage and papers checked by Mexican immigration; I figured it would be easy to talk them out of the actuality of my papers being long expired, but it wasn't. An officer was there who responded to me no more than another American tourist and all my humps and pleadings, and the lights in my eye notwithstanding, he didn't change his mind. I couldn't leave without turning back to *gobernación* (I knew while we went through all of this that it was a hoax, that they would threaten delay till I got really upset and then would hit on me for an immediate fine—oh, the workings of the Mexican mind!). So I decided not to throw my weight around, but to offer them money, and they took it, right up to the last cent I had, fifty dollars worth. It cost me to get out of Mexico, and I got on that plane bitter that Mexico sent me back as naked and lost as it had received me.

The plane settled down in Baltimore airfield, and I stepped off dizzy, with very little need to defend myself from people any more, I was fearless in the triviality of American physical day-to-day nothing. I drove with my father through the outskirts of Washington, D.C. and I thought it was a dream. There was no fear in talking to my father, only an unwillingness to talk too much and display to him my savage self and scare him out of his skin.

I felt a very great distance between myself and all this land and all these people. Everything that I had experienced was alive in me, open wounds that still breathed the compulsory air of Mexcity nights. Oh, let it all cry itself out. I took to crying in the immobile afternoon air of the United States, Washington, D.C.

Despite all this, I still had my plan and myth wrapped around me: this was just a stopping-over point, though the loss of my money to immigration officials blighted my hope of leaving immediately for Italy. I applied to the Italian Embassy right away for a visa, and I thought that those dark men there in the embassy were the only ones I had seen in Washington, D.C. who understood how I looked; I thought men in the States were a bunch of robots. I had my new pictures made for the embassy, and lay in bed long afternoons at my father's house waiting for Pedrito to arrive, not really wanting him, though missing a kind of romanticism and wondering what I would do if he didn't come. My father must have been a little afraid of me anyway, because he didn't make any comments about my trip to Italy being ridiculous, as I would have expected. The only bug was that he wanted to inspect my paintings, and I felt guilty about my actual lack of creative energy.

Pedrito arrived a week later and I immediately knew that he was a fool and I was stuck with a white elephant. He didn't call my house early in the morning when he arrived, so he had a taxi take him to a motel way south of town out in the woods, where the motel keeper milked him of his surviving money from the taxi ride, figuring from the way he acted he was some strange South American ambassador or something in the night arriving lost, and gave him nothing but the best, which of course Pedrito was used to having.

I had worked three days so we at least had twenty dollars to take us to New York, where hustling the New York streets awaited me as the only means to earn our passage to Italy.

So we went to New York and stayed for a week with my sister Lucy in Brooklyn. She wasn't at all shook by the strangeness of Pedrito, knowing the Spanish character as she did thoroughly. Pedrito immediately showed me what a burden on me he planned to be, and just sat around my sister's house all the time looking forward to meal time, and in truth I couldn't think of anything better to do either. The streets of New York were a scary thing for me, and I pondered in my mind a way to break into the scene, trying to figure the most likely district of New York to find the type of person I was used to hustling; feeling secretly that the type didn't exist in the States anyway. We spent the remainder of our money one night to go to a hotel where we sat together drinking, figuring that I would be seen by someone who could be considered a prospect, hoping that Pedrito would be seen by some rich old lady who would take a fall for his slick looks. (Which by then I had put down as the greasy Spanish type. I didn't even like to be near him any more, except that it had got to be a habit.) But nothing at all happened, till we got self-conscious spending our last small amounts of money for a specific purpose, whereas everyone else was just easily letting flow some cocktail relaxation before their dinner plans, and had no thought of money at all, and were not the least interested in us.

I couldn't figure abandoning Pedrito there at my sister's house, where she probably wouldn't know how to take care of him. I started looking for a place to stay in New York, thinking that independently we could make something of our situation. We got a room near Columbia University that was within taxi reach of the existing rich hotels, and kept up our belief that something good would happen soon.

New York City in the morning, Columbia students going by, Pedrito left behind in the room as I told him I was going for a walk. But more than that, I had thought of a way to get rid of him and wanted to walk around free in anticipation of it, and think it out. The sun was shining bright in the May afternoon; even the subways seemed friendly as I passed downtown into the village neighborhood, sick of being lonely, loneliness over, maybe I would see someone I knew, or walk by the place where Ray was staying.

I was dressed in blue jeans, going to the village, wow! It felt good to just walk the street again and not worry about who was looking at me or where I was going, just walking the afternoon street slowly. Felt good, and it didn't much matter what all was expected of me, for I knew best that it came and it went as slowly as I was walking, at least till the walk was over.

I didn't walk through the park, but went straight up 8th Street with the early summer heat making everything very friendly and communicative, so that even though I saw nobody I knew it was enough just to have been there before.

And I felt good, too! Walking along there, I knew I had my own self on my hands to deal with, and no ties at all to keep me from going in whatever direction I cared to travel in. This May afternoon I knew that my face was changed from years ago, that Rachel had come and gone telling a story of fractional twitches and new strains on my face which made me a whole different personality, bearing this one thing from day to day, and the disillusion. However I tried to combat it, it had happened, and that set a whole cloud on a face that knew most of its consciousness in expressing it. And I put all the make-up on over that, thinking that I could still control myself.

In spite of all these things it was a happy day, and I approached the corner where Sagamore's used to be in Cooper Square, not a dime in my pocket. Oh, Bowery Bum, things don't change much do they? Who's to answer me that one? And just at that moment, in that just-to-switch-about loneliness of the May afternoon, catching me shrinking away, wondering who to turn to from my loneliness, I heard my name (I had been walking with my head down, thinking) behind me, hesitantly, sounding familiar. I turned and saw Ray there, as natural as if it were meant to be, and felt a jump somewhere in my chest and thought it was fear. And God, the thought that I was away from him because I didn't love him? At that moment he put his hand around my waist, across from the new Five Spot, and I knew that it wasn't over, and shyly yet, for we had so much to talk about, let him do it and did nothing to contradict. But he took it away, self-conscious, and told me he didn't recognize me, and didn't I see him walk past, that I had looked right at him and didn't say a word. I denied it and told him I had been thinking. He immediately thought it was something weird, but didn't give a fuck in the slap-happy soon-to-be pot high together afternoon.

And when we kissed, wow! No, let me say it slowly: I asked Ray if he could give me ten dollars, he said yes, and wanted to know why, and I got hung up about having it immediately in my possession for I wanted to be sure of my escape to my mother. So there it was, whooped on me immediately, somehow Ray had a pretty thorough understanding of me by this time, and what's more, an impressive ten bucks. That left me free in time, because I intimated that otherwise I was looking for a hustle. And he told me to forget about hustling. When I asked him where the money would come from, he told me someone had laid some on him, that he had sold some pot for David M or something, all harmless and pretty and everything cool and O.K.

There was not much need to talk, the world was all full of beautiful things to see, I had Ray beside me and I was not lonesome any more, deep inside; there were all the external changes to be looked forward to, and the wait for some blast to fuse us (did I fear violence or lack of trust?). There was no time for negatives. Ray was staying where? "Oh, I am staying at several places, a couple of chicks' houses, but mostly at David M's where we run a kind of bachelor apartment together, let's go up there...."

So we did, into his back room there, front really, onto the street. My intuitions were right the one time earlier I had got the address walking by from Irving, and had known that if there were front windows in a pad Ray would be found in them watching the street, but the front windows were empty that time. Ray sat on the bed, showed me where he kept all the drawings I had done in Mexico, all the photographs of us two, all the new poetry he had written, an all-equipped writing room there in that apartment on East 12th Street.

Ray stuck a needle in his arm—amphetamine—and his face came up looking so strong, like voyages down under in those few seconds of complete introspection with the needle going in, and I knew it was good, and let myself be talked into it, and truly my eyes were opened. It went straight to my eyes, and the lids pushed apart and particles of air stimulated me to sight. And first we fucked, and I reserved this here out of respect mainly for girls who might get envious and discontented, and say to someone: if they went through that, and the result was that she achieved such a perfect fuck, just that one time (but it didn't stop! oh, be cool) then I say it's worth it. It was. I gave Ray back his ten dollars and decided to stay.

October 11, 1964

SELECTED DALKEY ARCHIVE PAPERBACKS

Petros Abatzoglou, *What Does Mrs. Freeman Want?*
Pierre Albert-Birot, *Grabinoulor.*
Yuz Aleshkovsky, *Kangaroo.*
Felipe Alfau, *Chromos.*
  Locos.
Ivan Ângelo, *The Celebration.*
  The Tower of Glass.
David Antin, *Talking.*
Alain Arias-Misson, *Theatre of Incest.*
Djuna Barnes, *Ladies Almanack.*
  Ryder.
John Barth, *LETTERS.*
  Sabbatical.
Donald Barthelme, *The King.*
  Paradise.
Svetislav Basara, *Chinese Letter.*
Mark Binelli, *Sacco and Vanzetti Must Die!*
Andrei Bitov, *Pushkin House.*
Louis Paul Boon, *Chapel Road.*
  Summer in Termuren.
Roger Boylan, *Killoyle.*
Ignácio de Loyola Brandão, *Teeth under the Sun.*
  Zero.
Bonnie Bremser, *Troia: Mexican Memoirs.*
Christine Brooke-Rose, *Amalgamemnon.*
Brigid Brophy, *In Transit.*
Meredith Brosnan, *Mr. Dynamite.*
Gerald L. Bruns,
  Modern Poetry and the Idea of Language.
Evgeny Bunimovich and J. Kates, eds.,
  Contemporary Russian Poetry: An Anthology.
Gabrielle Burton, *Heartbreak Hotel.*
Michel Butor, *Degrees.*
  Mobile.
  Portrait of the Artist as a Young Ape.
G. Cabrera Infante, *Infante's Inferno.*
  Three Trapped Tigers.
Julieta Campos, *The Fear of Losing Eurydice.*
Anne Carson, *Eros the Bittersweet.*
Camilo José Cela, *Christ versus Arizona.*
  The Family of Pascual Duarte.
  The Hive.
Louis-Ferdinand Céline, *Castle to Castle.*
  Conversations with Professor Y.
  London Bridge.
  North.
  Rigadoon.
Hugo Charteris, *The Tide Is Right.*
Jerome Charyn, *The Tar Baby.*
Marc Cholodenko, *Mordechai Schamz.*
Emily Holmes Coleman, *The Shutter of Snow.*
Robert Coover, *A Night at the Movies.*
Stanley Crawford, *Some Instructions to My Wife.*
Robert Creeley, *Collected Prose.*
René Crevel, *Putting My Foot in It.*
Ralph Cusack, *Cadenza.*
Susan Daitch, *L.C.*
  Storytown.
Nigel Dennis, *Cards of Identity.*
Peter Dimock,
  A Short Rhetoric for Leaving the Family.
Ariel Dorfman, *Konfidenz.*
Coleman Dowell, *The Houses of Children.*
  Island People.
  Too Much Flesh and Jabez.
Rikki Ducornet, *The Complete Butcher's Tales.*
  The Fountains of Neptune.
  The Jade Cabinet.
  Phosphor in Dreamland.
  The Stain.
  The Word "Desire."
William Eastlake, *The Bamboo Bed.*
  Castle Keep.
  Lyric of the Circle Heart.
Jean Echenoz, *Chopin's Move.*
Stanley Elkin, *A Bad Man.*
  Boswell: A Modern Comedy.
  Criers and Kibitzers, Kibitzers and Criers.
  The Dick Gibson Show.
  The Franchiser.
  George Mills.
  The Living End.
  The MacGuffin.
  The Magic Kingdom.
  Mrs. Ted Bliss.
  The Rabbi of Lud.
  Van Gogh's Room at Arles.
Annie Ernaux, *Cleaned Out.*

Lauren Fairbanks, *Muzzle Thyself.*
  Sister Carrie.
Leslie A. Fiedler,
  Love and Death in the American Novel.
Gustave Flaubert, *Bouvard and Pécuchet.*
Ford Madox Ford, *The March of Literature.*
Jon Fosse, *Melancholy.*
Max Frisch, *I'm Not Stiller.*
  Man in the Holocene.
Carlos Fuentes, *Christopher Unborn.*
  Distant Relations.
  Terra Nostra.
  Where the Air Is Clear.
Janice Galloway, *Foreign Parts.*
  The Trick Is to Keep Breathing.
William H. Gass, *A Temple of Texts.*
  The Tunnel.
  Willie Masters' Lonesome Wife.
Etienne Gilson, *The Arts of the Beautiful.*
  Forms and Substances in the Arts.
C. S. Giscombe, *Giscome Road.*
  Here.
Douglas Glover, *Bad News of the Heart.*
  The Enamoured Knight.
Witold Gombrowicz, *A Kind of Testament.*
Karen Elizabeth Gordon, *The Red Shoes.*
Georgi Gospodinov, *Natural Novel.*
Juan Goytisolo, *Count Julian.*
  Marks of Identity.
Patrick Grainville, *The Cave of Heaven.*
Henry Green, *Blindness.*
  Concluding.
  Doting.
  Nothing.
Jiří Gruša, *The Questionnaire.*
Gabriel Gudding, *Rhode Island Notebook.*
John Hawkes, *Whistlejacket.*
Aidan Higgins, *A Bestiary.*
  Bornholm Night-Ferry.
  Flotsam and Jetsam.
  Langrishe, Go Down.
  Scenes from a Receding Past.
  Windy Arbours.
Aldous Huxley, *Antic Hay.*
  Crome Yellow.
  Point Counter Point.
  Those Barren Leaves.
  Time Must Have a Stop.
Mikhail Iossel and Jeff Parker, eds., *Amerika:*
  Contemporary Russians View
  the United States.
Gert Jonke, *Geometric Regional Novel.*
Jacques Jouet, *Mountain R.*
Hugh Kenner, *The Counterfeiters.*
  Flaubert, Joyce and Beckett:
  The Stoic Comedians.
  Joyce's Voices.
Danilo Kiš, *Garden, Ashes.*
  A Tomb for Boris Davidovich.
Aiko Kitahara,
  The Budding Tree: Six Stories of Love in Edo.
Anita Konkka, *A Fool's Paradise.*
George Konrád, *The City Builder.*
Tadeusz Konwicki, *A Minor Apocalypse.*
  The Polish Complex.
Menis Koumandareas, *Koula.*
Elaine Kraf, *The Princess of 72nd Street.*
Jim Krusoe, *Iceland.*
Ewa Kuryluk, *Century 21.*
Violette Leduc, *La Bâtarde.*
Deborah Levy, *Billy and Girl.*
  Pillow Talk in Europe and Other Places.
José Lezama Lima, *Paradiso.*
Rosa Liksom, *Dark Paradise.*
Osman Lins, *Avalovara.*
  The Queen of the Prisons of Greece.
Alf Mac Lochlainn, *The Corpus in the Library.*
  Out of Focus.
Ron Loewinsohn, *Magnetic Field(s).*
D. Keith Mano, *Take Five.*
Ben Marcus, *The Age of Wire and String.*
Wallace Markfield, *Teitelbaum's Window.*
  To an Early Grave.
David Markson, *Reader's Block.*
  Springer's Progress.
  Wittgenstein's Mistress.
Carole Maso, *AVA.*

FOR A FULL LIST OF PUBLICATIONS, VISIT:
www.dalkeyarchive.com

SELECTED DALKEY ARCHIVE PAPERBACKS

LADISLAV MATEJKA AND KRYSTYNA POMORSKA, EDS., *Readings in Russian Poetics: Formalist and Structuralist Views.*
HARRY MATHEWS, *The Case of the Persevering Maltese: Collected Essays.*
Cigarettes.
The Conversions.
The Human Country: New and Collected Stories.
The Journalist.
My Life in CIA.
Singular Pleasures.
The Sinking of the Odradek Stadium.
Tlooth.
20 Lines a Day.
ROBERT L. MCLAUGHLIN, ED., *Innovations: An Anthology of Modern & Contemporary Fiction.*
HERMAN MELVILLE, *The Confidence-Man.*
STEVEN MILLHAUSER, *The Barnum Museum.*
In the Penny Arcade.
RALPH J. MILLS, JR., *Essays on Poetry.*
OLIVE MOORE, *Spleen.*
NICHOLAS MOSLEY, *Accident.*
Assassins.
Catastrophe Practice.
Children of Darkness and Light.
Experience and Religion.
The Hesperides Tree.
Hopeful Monsters.
Imago Bird.
Impossible Object.
Inventing God.
Judith.
Look at the Dark.
Natalie Natalia.
Serpent.
Time at War.
The Uses of Slime Mould: Essays of Four Decades.
WARREN F. MOTTE, JR., *Fables of the Novel: French Fiction since 1990.*
Oulipo: A Primer of Potential Literature.
YVES NAVARRE, *Our Share of Time.*
Sweet Tooth.
DOROTHY NELSON, *In Night's City.*
Tar and Feathers.
WILFRIDO D. NOLLEDO, *But for the Lovers.*
FLANN O'BRIEN, *At Swim-Two-Birds.*
At War.
The Best of Myles.
The Dalkey Archive.
Further Cuttings.
The Hard Life.
The Poor Mouth.
The Third Policeman.
CLAUDE OLLIER, *The Mise-en-Scène.*
PATRIK OUŘEDNÍK, *Europeana.*
FERNANDO DEL PASO, *Palinuro of Mexico.*
ROBERT PINGET, *The Inquisitory.*
Mahu or The Material.
Trio.
RAYMOND QUENEAU, *The Last Days.*
Odile.
Pierrot Mon Ami.
Saint Glinglin.
ANN QUIN, *Berg.*
Passages.
Three.
Tripticks.
ISHMAEL REED, *The Free-Lance Pallbearers.*
The Last Days of Louisiana Red.
Reckless Eyeballing.
The Terrible Threes.
The Terrible Twos.
Yellow Back Radio Broke-Down.
JEAN RICARDOU, *Place Names.*
JULIÁN RÍOS, *Larva: A Midsummer Night's Babel.*
Poundemonium.
AUGUSTO ROA BASTOS, *I the Supreme.*
JACQUES ROUBAUD, *The Great Fire of London.*
Hortense in Exile.
Hortense Is Abducted.
The Plurality of Worlds of Lewis.
The Princess Hoppy.

The Form of a City Changes Faster, Alas, Than the Human Heart.
Some Thing Black.
LEON S. ROUDIEZ, *French Fiction Revisited.*
VEDRANA RUDAN, *Night.*
LYDIE SALVAYRE, *The Company of Ghosts.*
Everyday Life.
The Lecture.
The Power of Flies.
LUIS RAFAEL SÁNCHEZ, *Macho Camacho's Beat.*
SEVERO SARDUY, *Cobra & Maitreya.*
NATHALIE SARRAUTE, *Do You Hear Them?*
Martereau.
The Planetarium.
ARNO SCHMIDT, *Collected Stories.*
Nobodaddy's Children.
CHRISTINE SCHUTT, *Nightwork.*
GAIL SCOTT, *My Paris.*
JUNE AKERS SEESE, *Is This What Other Women Feel Too?*
What Waiting Really Means.
AURELIE SHEEHAN, *Jack Kerouac Is Pregnant.*
VIKTOR SHKLOVSKY, *Knight's Move.*
A Sentimental Journey: Memoirs 1917-1922.
Energy of Delusion: A Book on Plot.
Theory of Prose.
Third Factory.
Zoo, or Letters Not about Love.
JOSEF ŠKVORECKÝ, *The Engineer of Human Souls.*
CLAUDE SIMON, *The Invitation.*
GILBERT SORRENTINO, *Aberration of Starlight.*
Blue Pastoral.
Crystal Vision.
Imaginative Qualities of Actual Things.
Mulligan Stew.
Pack of Lies.
Red the Fiend.
The Sky Changes.
Something Said.
Splendide-Hôtel.
Steelwork.
Under the Shadow.
W. M. SPACKMAN, *The Complete Fiction.*
GERTRUDE STEIN, *Lucy Church Amiably.*
The Making of Americans.
A Novel of Thank You.
PIOTR SZEWC, *Annihilation.*
STEFAN THEMERSON, *Hobson's Island.*
The Mystery of the Sardine.
Tom Harris.
JEAN-PHILIPPE TOUSSAINT, *Television.*
DUMITRU TSEPENEAG, *Vain Art of the Fugue.*
ESTHER TUSQUETS, *Stranded.*
DUBRAVKA UGRESIC, *Lend Me Your Character.*
Thank You for Not Reading.
MATI UNT, *Things in the Night.*
ELOY URROZ, *The Obstacles.*
LUISA VALENZUELA, *He Who Searches.*
PAUL VERHAEGHEN, *Omega Minor.*
MARJA-LIISA VARTIO, *The Parson's Widow.*
BORIS VIAN, *Heartsnatcher.*
AUSTRYN WAINHOUSE, *Hedyphagetica.*
PAUL WEST, *Words for a Deaf Daughter & Gala.*
CURTIS WHITE, *America's Magic Mountain.*
The Idea of Home.
Memories of My Father Watching TV.
Monstrous Possibility: An Invitation to Literary Politics.
Requiem.
DIANE WILLIAMS, *Excitability: Selected Stories.*
Romancer Erector.
DOUGLAS WOOLF, *Wall to Wall.*
Ya! & John-Juan.
PHILIP WYLIE, *Generation of Vipers.*
MARGUERITE YOUNG, *Angel in the Forest.*
Miss MacIntosh, My Darling.
REYOUNG, *Unbabbling.*
ZORAN ŽIVKOVIĆ, *Hidden Camera.*
LOUIS ZUKOFSKY, *Collected Fiction.*
SCOTT ZWIREN, *God Head.*

FOR A FULL LIST OF PUBLICATIONS, VISIT:
www.dalkeyarchive.com